THE HISCOX

STANDARD

BAPTIST MANUAL

D1564745

THE HISCOX STANDARD BAPTIST MANUAL

EDWARD T. HISCOX

JUDSON PRESS ®   *Valley Forge*

THE HISCOX STANDARD BAPTIST MANUAL

Copyright © 1965

JUDSON PRESS

Valley Forge, PA 19482-0851

International Standard Book No. 0-8170-0340-1
Library of Congress Catalog Card No. 65-22002

PRINTED IN THE U.S.A.
10 09 08 07 06 05 04 03 02 01 00 99 98 97
20 19 18 17 16 15

CONTENTS

FOREWORD

THE writings of the late Edward T. Hiscox (1814-1901) have been a favorite among countless thousands of Baptists in the United States, ever since the first publication of his *Baptist Church Directory* in 1859. During his lifetime, Dr. Hiscox made every effort to keep his book current, revising it frequently, and publishing various smaller volumes from time to time to extract those materials which would be useful in shorter form. Finally, toward the end of the century, he returned to his manuscripts for a thoroughgoing revision, which ensued in two completely new books. These were very similar to each other in the ideas presented and in the range of subjects treated; they differed principally in that one covered the material much more intensively than the other. The shorter version, known as *The Standard Manual for Baptist Churches*, was published in 1890, and the more comprehensive volume, *The New Directory for Baptist Churches*, appeared in the year 1894.

Because of many changes which have occurred in church life with the passage of time, it became necessary for The Judson Press to prepare a revision of *The New Directory for Baptist Churches,* which was published in 1964, with the approval of the Hiscox family, under the title, *The Hiscox Guide for Baptist Churches.* In that volume an effort was made to preserve as much as possible of Dr. Hiscox's original work, revising, adding, or substituting only those materials which would make the book of maximum usefulness to present-day churches.

So favorable has been the reaction to *The Hiscox Guide* that the editors have now deemed it wise to prepare a briefer and less expensive version which is here presented as *The Hiscox Standard Baptist Manual.* In so doing they have followed the lead of Dr. Hiscox, whose original *Standard Manual* was an abbreviated version of the earlier *Directory.*

The present volume is identical with the eight basic chapters of *The Hiscox Guide,* plus the New Hampshire Confession of Faith. Practically all of the useful supplementary materials contained in more than 100 pages of appendices in the larger book are omitted here. For those who wish a more thorough reference, therefore, *The Hiscox Guide* is to be preferred.

FRANK T. HOADLEY
Book Editor, The Judson Press

Valley Forge, Pa.
May 1, 1965

CHAPTER I

THE NATURE OF THE CHURCH

A Christian church, according to the point of
view traditionally held by Baptists, is a company of
regenerate persons, baptized on profession of faith
in Christ; united in covenant for worship, instruction, the observance of Christian ordinances, and for
such service as the gospel requires; recognizing and
accepting Christ as their supreme lord and lawgiver,
and taking the New Testament as a divinely inspired
record and therefore a trustworthy, authoritative,
and all-sufficient rule of faith and practice.

A. Meaning of the Word

The English word "church" (Scottish, *kirk*; German, *kirche*; Danish, *kyrke*; Swedish, *kyrka*; Russian,
zerkow) is literally derived from the Greek *kuriakon*
—"belonging to the Lord." *Kuriakon*, however, is
not the word used in the New Testament; rather,
the word which has been translated "church" is
ekklesia.

Ekklesia is composed of *ek* ("from" or "out of") and *kaleo* ("to call") "called out from." It denotes a company, or assembly of persons, called out, selected, chosen, and separated from a larger company. According to the usages of Greek civil life, the *ekklesia* was, as the lexicons define it, "an assembly of citizens called together for deliberative purposes; a legislative assembly, called to discuss the affairs of state." It was an orderly and organized assembly, consisting of those possessing the rights of citizenship, for the consideration of public affairs and the enactment and enforcement of laws pertaining to the public welfare—as distinguished from the common populace at large, an incidental gathering, or a disorderly crowd of people.

Still true to its original classical idea and scope of meaning, when the word was adopted into Christian literature and applied to higher and more sacred uses, it designated a company called out from the world, elected, chosen, and separated—*eklektoi*, the elected, the faithful, called to be saints. And thus a selected and separated company, to constitute "the kingdom of Christ," "the church of the living God," the "people of God." Here, also, we have the further idea, fundamental to its primitive meaning, of an organized company, with laws, officers, and ordinances for the orderly transaction of affairs, and the performance of service contemplated in their calling and institution.

The word *ekklesia* is found 115 times in the New Testament. In 110 of these instances it has reference to the institution known as the church. In three instances it is used in a non-Christian sense, being applied to the assembly gathered at Ephesus on the occasion of the riot incited against Paul and his associates (Acts 19:32, 39, 41). Notice, however, that the excited and riotous multitude was the *oklos*—a crowd, a confused and disorderly multitude, Acts 19:33, and not the *ekklesia*, which was the official and authoritative assembly to which such cases of popular disturbance and disorder were appealed for suppression and settlement. In two cases this word is used in a Jewish sense, being applied to ancient Israel as God's chosen and separated people. In the address of Stephen before his accusers, when referring to Mosaic history, he said: "This is he that was in the church (*ekklesia*) in the wilderness, with the angel which spake to him" (Acts 7:38); and in the Epistle to the Hebrews there is a citation from the Twenty-second Psalm: "I will declare thy name unto my brethren; in the midst of the church (*ekklesia*) will I sing praise unto thee (Heb. 2:12; Ps. 22:22). Here the word expresses the idea that the seed of Abraham constituted a distinct congregation, called out and separated from all other peoples and races, organized under a polity peculiarly their own, with distinct laws, ordinances, and services.

In the Christian sense the word *ekklesia* has a two-fold significance in the New Testament. *First*, it is used in its primary and literal sense, to designate a visible, local congregation of Christian disciples, meeting for worship, instruction, and service. *Second*, it is used in a secondary and figurative sense, to designate the invisible, universal company, including all of God's true people on earth and in heaven. There is, then, the visible, local church, and the invisible, universal church. In the latter case the word represents a conception of the mind, having no real existence in time or place, and not a historical fact, being only an ideal multitude without organization, without action, and without corporate being.

Of the 110 instances in which *ekklesia* is rendered "church" in the New Testament, more than ninety are applied to a visible, local congregation, or company of disciples, meeting in a given place, for a given purpose. This is the primary and literal significance of the word. Thus it is said, "Paul called the elders of the church," "the church of God at Corinth," "the seven churches of Asia," "the church of Ephesus," "the churches of Galatia." But when it is said, "Christ also loved the church, and gave himself for it, that he might present it to himself a glorious church" (Eph. 5:25, 27), it presumably refers to no particular congregation of believers, but to the entire company of the saved—the universal, invisible church. In the same way is interpreted the much-quoted declaration of Jesus: "On this rock will I build my church (Matt. 16:18). Also, "To the intent that now . . . might be known by the church the manifold wisdom of God" (Eph. 3:10); "He is the head of the body, the church" (Col. 1:18); and "The general assembly and church of the firstborn, which are written in heaven" (Heb. 12:23). These, with a few other passages, are supposed to refer not to any localized congregations of believers, but to the universal fellowship of the faithful.

B. Historic Definitions

All the various Christian communions, both ancient and modern, have, in their dogmatic symbols, more or less fully given their conception of a true church. These definitions are found in their standard creeds and confessions of faith; and it is to be observed that they all assume to start with the New Testament idea. But, as they proceed, they more and more diverge, and complicate the primitive simplicity with their ecclesiastical surroundings, their educational prepossessions, or with what trusted authority decides a church ought to be, rather than what it is.

The Latin Church gives this definition of a church:

> The company of Christians knit together by the profession of the same faith, and the communion of the same sacraments, under the government of lawful pastors, and especially of the Roman bishop, as the only vicar of Christ on earth.—*Bellarmine De Eccl. Mil., III, 2.*

The Greek Church gives this definition:

> The church is a divinely instituted community of men united by the orthodox faith, the law of God, the hierarchy, and the sacraments.—*Full Catec. of the Orthodox Est. Church.*

The Church of England defines after this manner:

> A congregation of faithful men, in which the pure Word of God is preached, and the sacraments duly administered according to Christ's ordinances, in all those things that of necessity are requisite to the same. —*Thirty-nine Articles, Art. XIX.*

The Augsburg Confession has the following:

A congregation of saints, in which the gospel is purely preached, and the sacraments are rightly administered.—*Aug. Conf., Art. VII.*

The Helvetic Confession states it thus:

The church is a community of believers, or saints, gathered out of the world, whose distinction is to know and to worship, through the Word and by the Spirit, the true God in Christ the Savior.—*Helv. Conf., Art. XVII.*

The Belgic Confession gives this definition:

A true congregation or assembly of all faithful Christians, who look for their salvation only from Jesus Christ, as being washed by his blood and sanctified by his Spirit.—*Belg. Conf., Art. XXVII.*

The Saxon Confession defines in these words:

A congregation of men embracing the gospel of Christ, and rightly using the sacraments.—*Saxon Conf., Art. XII.*

The Scottish Confession puts it in these words:

The church is a society of the elect of all ages and countries both Jews and Gentiles; this is the catholic, or universal church. This church is invisible, and known only to God.—*Scot. Conf., Art. XVI.*

The Westminster Assembly's definition is this:

Particular churches in the primitive times were made up of visible saints, viz., of such as being of age, professing faith in Christ, according to the rules of faith and life taught by Christ and his apostles, and of their children.—*West. Assem. Directory.*

Baptists have attached less importance to creedal statements than most other denominations. Nevertheless they, too, have some historic documents which they respect and use, but to which they are not bound.

The London Confession of Faith, issued by seven

Baptist churches in London in 1644 as a vindication from the aspersions and calumnies of their opponents and enemies, defines a church as follows:

> Christ hath here on earth a spiritual kingdom which is the church, which he hath purchased and redeemed to himself, as a peculiar inheritance: which church . . . is a company of visible saints, called and separated from the world by the Word and Spirit of God, to the visible profession of the faith of the gospel; being baptized into that faith, and joined to the Lord, and each other, by mutual agreement, in the practical enjoyment of the ordinances commanded by Christ their head and king.—*Art. XXXIII.*[1]

The Second London Confession, put forth by the elders and brethren of many Baptist congregations in London, 1677, evidently based on that of 1644, and adopted by the "General Assembly" of ministers and delegates of more than one hundred "baptized churches," in 1689, says:

> The Lord Jesus Christ calleth out of the world unto himself, through the ministry of his word, by his Spirit, those that are given unto him by his Father, that they may walk before him in all the ways of obedience, which he prescribeth to them in his word. Those thus called he commandeth to walk together in particular societies, or churches, for their mutual edification, and the due performance of that public worship which he requireth of them in the world. The members of these churches are saints by calling, visibly manifesting and evidencing . . . their obedience unto that call of Christ; and do willingly consent to walk together according to the appointment of Christ, giving up themselves to the Lord, and one to another, by the will of God, in

[1] William L. Lumpkin (ed.), *Baptist Confessions of Faith.* Valley Forge: The Judson Press, 1959. Page 165.

professed subjection to the ordinances of the gospel.—
Chap. XXVI, secs. 5, 6.[2]

The New Hampshire Confession, 1833, more
briefly gives the following definition:

> A visible church of Christ is a congregation of bap-
> tized believers, associated by covenant in the faith and
> fellowship of the gospel; observing the ordinances of
> Christ, governed by his laws, and exercising the gifts,
> rights, and privileges invested in them by his word.—
> *Art. XIII.*[3]

C. New Testament Analogies

The church is not infrequently spoken of in the
New Testament in certain analogies, showing the
nature, purpose, and relations of this institution.
The fact that analogies are not intended as logical
definitions, and only incidentally define, makes them
perhaps the more interesting.

"And gave him to be the head over all things to
the church, which is his body" (Eph. 1:22-23). Christ
is the head, and the church his body. This is equally
true of the church universal and invisible, and of the
church local and visible—head over all things, and
in all respects. The head is the intelligent director,
the authoritative lawgiver, to the body, and furnishes
the will-force for active obedience. The church as
the body is to obey the directions and to execute the

---

[2] *Ibid.*, page 286. In 1742 The Philadelphia Association adopted
this with some additions and changes, and this version is known in
the United States as The Philadelphia Confession.

[3] *Ibid.*, p. 365. This confession received many revisions, particularly at the hands of J. Newton Brown and Dr. Hiscox. The
reference above is to the 1833 text. Dr. Hiscox's version of the
entire New Hampshire Confession appears in Appendix B.

authoritative mandates of Christ, the head. The figure indicates the intimate, sensitive, and sacred relation existing between Christ and his people. Also observe, there are not many heads, but one only—Christ.

"Husbands, love your wives, even as Christ also loved the church, and gave himself for it" (Eph. 5:25). Here the relation existing between Christ and the church is illustrated by the relation of husband and wife, intimate, tender, affectionate, sacred, through which each fulfills the other.

"The house of God, which is the church of the living God, the pillar and ground of the truth" (1 Tim. 3:15). The pillar supports the upper portion of the building. The ground, literally foundation, is that on which the building rests, and upon which it is constructed. Thus, while in an emphatic sense Christ is the only foundation for the faith of saints, the hope of souls, yet in a very important sense does the church become the support of all Christian endeavor, whether for the education and growth of its own members or the spread of the gospel and the evangelization of the world. As a historical fact the churches of Christ have acted this part and served this purpose, and are now serving it—indeed, this is the very end for which they were instituted.

"Know ye not that ye are the temple of God, and that the Spirit of God dwelleth in you?" (1 Cor. 3:9-17). This is true, in a very important sense, of each individual Christian. But here it is declared true of the Corinthian church. The Apostle asserts that he has laid the foundation of the edifice, and others have built upon it. He declares the building to be holy, and cautions them not to defile this sanctuary. The abiding presence of the Spirit in a church gives importance to its existence, and efficacy to its ministrations. As a mere human organization it would not rise above the level of other moral and benevolent institutions. But the divine element enables it to fulfill its sacred purpose.

"As we have therefore opportunity, let us do good to all, especially unto them who are of the household of faith" (Gal. 6:10). Here the household represents the church in the Apostle's mind, a family, where mutual affection should rule; the members caring for each other's good, bearing one another's burdens, and guiding each other in Christian growth.

"Now, therefore, ye are no more strangers and foreigners, but fellow-citizens with the saints, and of the household of God" (Eph. 2:19). Here is a double metaphor. The church is likened to a state, a commonwealth, of which the members have been made citizens. They are now no longer strangers, temporarily sojourning, but naturalized and permanently abiding, entitled to all the immunities of citizens native born. And then, in a narrowed circle, but a more intimate and sacred relationship, they are represented as members of the holy family of God the Father.

In the closing chapter of the Revelation we have the church idea brought to view in a somewhat strange commingling of figures. But it is the church triumphant; and the unusual mixing of the metaphors gives a strange and vivid picturesqueness and beauty to the concept. The church is pictured here both as a bride and as a city, and Christ as a bridegroom and as a lamb: "And I John saw the holy city, new Jerusalem, coming down from God, out of heaven, prepared as a bride adorned for her husband. . . . And there came unto me one of the seven angels . . . saying, 'Come hither, I will show thee the bride, the Lamb's wife.' And he carried me away in the spirit to a great and high mountain, and showed me that great city, the holy Jerusalem, descending out of heaven from God" (Rev. 21:2, 9, 10).

The purity, beauty, and glory of the redeemed are implied in the bridal relation: in the affection of the Lamb, who is the Bridegroom, and his joy at the final reception of his bride, so beautiful, for whom he had suffered so much, and waited so long, that he might present her to himself, "a glorious church, not having spot or wrinkle, or any such thing" (Eph. 5:27). The added concept of a city, representing the company of glorified saints, may imply the transcendent glory of the final habitation of the righteous, in which the church triumphant shall be orderly and active as well as blissful and glorious, under the joyous and loving reign of their Lord, the prince of life, the one who is "the King eternal, immortal, invisible."

Thus the teachings of Scripture as to the church show the peculiar place in human society which this sacred brotherhood holds, and explain the redemptive purpose which, in God's mercy to a lost world, it was designed to serve.

D. Church and State

The Christian church is the only divinely organized society among men. It was instituted for a purpose by Christ, who gave to it laws and methods by which to accomplish its sacred mission, and who still retains headship and kinship over it. Each local church constitutes a body politic in a spiritual realm; in the world, but not of it; being able to maintain its existence and discharge its functions in all conditions of social and civil life, under all forms of human government.

Members of the church have all the rights, privileges, and immunities of any citizens under civil government, and owe allegiance to the nation in which they live, in all matters temporal, so long as such allegiance does not interfere with their perfect obedience to the claims of Christ. But if human laws and the demands of human governments contravene the divine claim, or in any way interfere with the rights of conscience or religious faith, and the freedom of belief and worship, then God is to be obeyed rather than man. His claims are supreme, and annihilate all rival claims. "Render to Caesar the things that are Caesar's, and to God the things that are God's" (Mark 12:17). Christian men should be good and law-abiding citizens, unless obedience to human law demands a violation of divine law. Their fealty to the higher law must be prompt and unquestioned. "Submit yourselves to every ordinance of man, for the Lord's sake; whether it be to the king as supreme, or unto governors, as unto them that are sent by him for the punishment of evildoers, and for the praise of them that do well. For so is the will of God, that with well doing ye may put to silence the ignorance of foolish men" (1 Peter 2:13-15). As to things spiritual, the state has no right of control over them. Matters of conscience, faith, and worship the civil power has no right to meddle with, so long as the government is not injured, nor the rights of others put in jeopardy by their exercise.

E. THE CHURCH IN THE WORLD

The nature of a church is very different from that of other societies and associations. Its members may be connected with other organizations, whose objects contemplate the furtherance of commerce, literature, science, or the arts; they may be moral, philanthropic, and even religious. But they do not reach the high ideal of the church's vocation, nor fill the broad sphere of the church's mission. That is no less than the glory of God and the salvation of souls. Fellowship in such other associations will be consistent and harmless—it may be even commendable—providing the objects they seek, and the methods by which they are sought, be consistent with Christian morals; and providing, also, their duties to these in no way interfere with their duties to and usefulness in, the church, whose claims are first and most imperative. In such other associations good may be accomplished by the wider diffusion of intelligence, the cultivation of social morals and public virtue, the relief of human suffering, and the advancement of civilization.

All these aims are good, and all good men should encourage them. But all these aims are contemplated by a Christian church, and can and will be better reached by a church, if true to its calling and mission, than by any other society. Beyond and above all these, remains the one special and unique object of the church's life, which all other societies lack: a regenerated humanity, in order to constitute the ultimate "church of the firstborn, which are written in heaven" (Heb. 12:23). Did not he who founded the church, who knew what was in man and who understood the world he came to save, who gave himself to restore the divine image in man and the divine authority over man, know what sort of organized endeavor, what kind of a society would be best adapted to accomplish the simple but sublime object contemplated? Every effort at social virtue and moral reform should find its best example and its most efficient advocacy in the church of God. It would be a shame for those who are expressly set forth to be the "light of the world" and the "salt of the earth" to fall below the standard of goodness in the secular world. Then would they no longer be "holding forth the word of life."

F. The Authority of Churches

All associations of men are supposed to possess as much authority as may be needful to control their members within the limits of their associational relations, to guard their organizations against perversion and disaster, and to accomplish the purposes for which they exist. This authority they have the consequent right to exercise, and power to enforce. It is derived either from voluntary compact, where each individual surrenders to the body a part of his personal freedom of action, or else is conferred by some external and superior authority. The authority of churches is mainly of the latter type.

Persons uniting with a church surrender voluntarily some personal prerogatives to the organic whole. But such personally surrendered prerogatives constitute but a small part of the church's authority. Its chief authority is given by Christ alone. The state cannot bestow it: Neither legislatures, nor courts of civil jurisdiction, nor princes, nor parliaments can bestow or annul the divine charter by right of which the churches of Christ exist and act. Likewise, that authority cannot emanate from any ecclesiastical source, since all ecclesiastical powers grow out of the churches, and are created by them.

This authority a church can exercise on none but its own members. It can bring the moral force of persuasion, of consistent living, and of Christian character, to bear on all around, as indeed it should; but as to authoritative administration, it can claim no right of interference with any except those with whom it holds covenant relations in the fellowship of the body. Said the Apostle to the Corinthians, "For what have I to do to judge them also that are without? Do not ye judge them that are within?" (1 Cor. 5:12). Nor can a church exercise authority over its own members in any respect except as to spiritual concerns. With their personal rights and duties as members of society, it cannot interfere. It cannot dictate what they shall eat or drink, or wherewithal they shall be clothed; what business they shall pursue, what associations they shall keep, what privileges they may enjoy; *except* that in all these they shall do nothing which shall be inconsistent with their position and profession as Christians; nothing that shall harm or hinder the gospel of Christ; nothing that shall destroy their influence for good, place a stumbling-block in the way of unconverted men, or cast a reproach on the Christian name. And of all these questions the church has the right to judge. The sphere of a church's authority is therefore distinctively and exclusively moral and spiritual.

Nor yet can a church dominate the faith or conscience of its members. With such personal religious liberty no man, or combination of men, has a right to interfere. For such liberty and its lawful exercise each one is responsible to God alone. The church's authority goes not so far. It can and should secure harmony in the faith and fellowship of the body, but complete doctrinal conformity is not its goal.

No church can exercise discipline upon another, or for another, or interfere in any way with another's disciplinary acts, but churches hold relations of comity and fraternal courtesy with each other. In the exchange of courtesies, churches dismiss members by letter to each other, and receive those dismissed; respect each other's disciplinary acts, but are not bound by them. Pastors exchange pulpits. Churches unite fraternally in associations for missionary and other Christian work of mutual concern.

G. Starting a New Church

Churches are constituted by voluntary covenant on the part of those who wish to become members. The constitution of a church, strictly speaking, is to be found in the New Testament only, as regards both faith and practice. It is customary, however, for individual churches to have constitutions in which New Testament principles are formulated in terms of the local church needs. And though no church and no church member is asked to sign them, or is required to pledge allegiance to them, yet a general and substantial assent and conformity to them is expected, in order that harmony in the churches and among the churches may be secured.

The process by which new churches are constituted is very simple. The necessity for, and the practicability of, organizing one, must be decided by those who are to constitute it, and who are to bear the expense and the responsibility of its support. These may be persons belonging to some other church or churches, who find themselves living where there is none, but where one is believed to be needed, and where the increase of population shows a need for increased religious opportunities. After mature deliberation on the part of such persons, meeting together for consultation, considering all sides of the question, securing advice from wise and experienced sources, including the association or convention with which the proposed church will be likely to affiliate, with much prayer for divine direction, when general agreement has been secured, a meeting is finally called for the organization. Prior to the meeting, a committee should draft a proposed constituting act and church covenant. A proposed constitution and by-laws may also be drafted at this time, together with articles of faith, if desired.[4]

Before the organization actually takes place, however, such persons as propose to constitute the body, should procure letters from the churches of which they are members, given *for the purpose of forming a new church*. Should there be among them persons who have been members of other churches, but have for any reason lost their membership without special fault of their own, who are living consistent Christian lives, they can, by consent of the company, be admitted as members by statement of Christian experience. Others may be admitted by baptism on profession of their faith in Christ.

The first actions of the constituting meeting, following the opening prayer, would be the election of a temporary moderator to insure the orderly conduct of the meeting, and of a temporary clerk to guarantee the keeping of accurate and adequate records.

The constituting act itself would properly and appropriately take place in the unanimous voting— perhaps by rising—of a resolution like this:

[4] At this point the present text departs from the recommendations of Dr. Hiscox, who did not consider a constitution and by-laws to be necessary. Twentieth-century custom, however, heavily favors the use of such documents. (See, for example, Maring and Hudson's *A Baptist Manual of Polity and Practice.* Asquith's *Church Officers at Work,* and McNutt's *Polity and Practice in Baptist Churches.*) On the other hand, the use of Articles of Faith, strongly recommended by Hiscox, is much less common today.

"*Resolved,* That, guided as we believe by the Holy Spirit, and relying on the blessing of God, we do here and now by this act constitute ourselves a church of Jesus Christ to perform his service and to be governed by his will, as revealed in the New Testament."

Other documents which have been prepared in advance by the committee, such as the covenant, this constitution, the by-laws, and (if desired) the articles of faith, should be considered next. Ample opportunity should be provided for free discussion, and for amendment when the group believes such to be the will of God. Upon approval of these, permanent officers of the new church should be elected, in accordance with its constitution, and a pastor should be called as soon thereafter as possible. Prayer for strength, guidance, and blessing upon the newly constituted church should follow.

It is customary for a new church to petition the local Baptist association for recognition and acceptance into membership. At this time the association may examine their doctrines, inquire into the circumstances and reasons for their organization, so as to be able to express approval of their course, and certify to the member churches that the new body is a regularly constituted church of the same faith.

It is customary to hold some public religious service suitable to the occasion, calculated to give encouragement in their enterprise to the new church and to assure them of the fellowship and sympathy of sister churches. This may be a part of the annual association meeting, or may be a separate occasion including an appropriate sermon, a charge to the church, and the extending of the hand of fellowship by an officer of the association.

NOTE 1.—The formation of new churches as the outgrowth and fruit of strife and dissension in older ones should be avoided and discountenanced, except in extreme cases. Careful observation proves that very few churches so constituted ever attain to any considerable degree of prosperity or usefulness.

NOTE 2.—If an association should decline to recognize a newly constituted church, deeming the organization unwise and uncalled for, still that church would have the right to maintain its organization and to continue its work and its worship. It would seldom, however, be wise to proceed against the wisdom and advice of pastors and members of other churches in an association. If, however, the counsel of the association has been sought in the early stages of planning for the new church, such an impasse is not likely to occur.

H. Disbanding a Church

It sometimes happens, under stress of circumstances, that it becomes needful, or at least seems wise, to abandon church organizations and to transfer the efforts made for their support to new fields, or to a union with other churches. It is always a matter of serious concern thus to remove the candlestick out of its place, and such a course should be determined on only after long consideration, much prayer, and consultation with wise and unbiased brethren. But duty may require that it shall be done. Where complicated and inveterate troubles in the body have been so long continued as to discourage all hope of further usefulness, the only resort may be to disband, and the members go into other churches.

Of the wisdom and propriety of such a step the body itself must be the judge, with all the light it can obtain; and since this step will most likely be opposed by some, the question must be finally decided by a majority of the members, as in other cases. There are some things, however, that majorities even cannot rightfully do, and they must proceed cautiously.

1. Each member has an inalienable right to all the immunities of church membership, whether moral, spiritual, social, or otherwise; which rights cannot be abrogated or alienated, and must be regarded as sacred. If the church be disbanded, therefore, letters must be given to all the members, which will secure them admission to other churches without loss of position or privilege.

2. There are rights of property also to be considered, if the church holds property purchased or given for religious uses. The deed by which such property is held, or the charter by which the church has become a legal corporation for the purpose of holding and controlling temporalities, would have to be well understood, so that such property might not be lost, or diverted to other uses than those for which it was given or purchased. The laws of the state, and the decisions of courts would have to be consulted, so that such property would still be used according to its original design.

3. If a church be disbanded, and absolutely dissolved, and a new one constituted by some of the same people, and to occupy the same building, the

new one cannot automatically hold the property, retain the officers, perpetuate the history, or claim the immunities of the old one, but must begin anew. Legal counsel should be obtained if the new group wishes to secure title to hold the property of the church which has been disbanded.

The process by which the organization is disbanded, or dissolved, is very simple. After all preliminary preparations are attended to—for no church acts can be performed after the final act of dissolution has been passed—letters having been voted to its members, and the clerk authorized to give such letters to any person who may subsequently appear, and have right to them; then a simple vote, "that we do here and now, by this act, disband as a church, and cease to exist as a corporate and covenant organization," will accomplish the purpose. What disposition shall be made of the records, of any furniture, or other effects belonging to them, would previously have been determined.[5]

[5] It is suggested that records be preserved permanently through the auspices of the American Baptist Historical Society, 1100 South Goodman St., Rochester, N. Y., or in some other historical library recommended by the association or state convention with which the disbanding church has been affiliated.

CHAPTER II

CHURCH MEMBERSHIP

It is sometimes said that a church is a *voluntary society*. This is true in a sense, but only with an explanation. It is true in that no external force or authority can compel the relation of membership to be formed or dissolved. Likewise, the church itself can compel no one to unite with it, nor can the individual oblige the body to receive him. But it is not merely optional whether or not a believer identifies himself with the household of faith. He is under moral obligation to do that. It is for his own spiritual good to do it; it is one of the appointed means of grace; the church needs his presence and influence, and the cause of truth is furthered by the combined Christian influence and effort of many. All are under law to Christ, and are bound by sacred obligations to obey and please him. He has ordained that his followers should associate themselves in these brotherhoods of faith and affection. A church, therefore is more than a voluntary society; it is a society under law to Christ.

Church membership thus becomes a question of grave moment, and should be carefully studied and well understood.

A. Conditions of Membership

What are the scriptural qualifications for citizenship in this spiritual kingdom, for brotherhood in the family of the faithful? These conditions are *four*: (1) a regenerate heart, (2) a confession of faith, (3) the reception of baptism, and (4) a Christian life.

1. *A Regenerate Heart*

If our churches are to fulfill their mission, remain true to their traditions, and honor their apostolic pretensions, they must insist, with unabated vigor, on a *regenerate membership*. Nor must they insist on it in theory only, but take every precaution to maintain it in practice.

This position, however, is one with which many Christians do not agree, claiming that nothing more than good moral character and a serious disposition to receive religious instruction should be demanded in candidates for church membership. By this practice the broad distinction between the church and the world is diminished or obliterated, the salt loses its savor, and the city set on a hill to that extent is hid, and ceases to be a monument of grace to men.

The teachings of the New Testament are emphatic on this point. Both Jesus and his apostles made it clear that his kingdom was not of this world, and those who constituted it were such as are born of the Spirit. The first churches, both Jewish and Gentile, were not indiscriminately gathered, but were *called out* from the masses of the people on a confession of faith in Christ, and on a spiritual change which betokened a regenerate nature. Such was the case at Pentecost, and subsequently it was "the saved" who were added to the churches. So was it at Samaria, Antioch, Ephesus, Corinth, Philippi—everywhere.

The church at Rome, for example, was addressed as "Beloved of God, called to be saints" (Rom. 1:7). And Paul reminds these same disciples of their former condition, "when ye were servants of sin," and contrasts it with their present condition: "But now, being made free from sin, and become servants to God, ye have your fruit unto holiness, and the end everlasting life" (Rom. 6:20, 22). The salutation to the Corinthians is, "Unto the church of God, which is at Corinth, to them that are sanctified in Christ Jesus, called to be saints" (1 Cor. 1:2). Peter, addressing the early Christians, says: "Ye also, as lively stones, are built up a spiritual house, an holy priesthood, to offer up spiritual sacrifices, acceptable to God, by Jesus Christ." And further, he declares: "But ye are a chosen generation, a royal priesthood, an holy nation, a peculiar people; that ye should show forth the praises of him who hath called you out of darkness into his marvelous light" (1 Peter 2:5, 9). The unvarying tone of New Testament utterance is the same. Those gathered in fraternal fellowship to constitute the churches of our Lord are such as have been called out of darkness into light, and from the power of Satan unto God. Once were they darkness, now are they light in the Lord.

2. A Confession of Faith

The bond of fellowship among Christians is the love of Christ, binding all in a common experience, a common hope, and a common sympathy to the Cross, the one common center of their new life. In order to make this fellowship real and personal to each, the newcomer who seeks admission to their company must give them evidence that he, too, has been born of the Spirit, and become an heir of God. How is he to give this evidence? By a confession to that effect, and by such change in character and conduct on his part as he is able to show. Without this, no evidence of fitness for membership with the disciples becomes apparent, and no fraternal fellowship is begotten.

This confession of faith is made verbally, by a declaration of the great change which has transpired. "With the heart man believeth unto righteousness, and with the mouth confession is made unto salvation" (Rom. 10:10). Without a confession of saving faith in Christ, and a profession of pardon and peace through the blood of the Covenant, there can be no spiritual fellowship, and membership in the church would be little more than a pretense.

3. The Reception of Baptism

Especially is a confession of faith to be made in baptism. A regenerate heart constitutes the spiritual qualification for church membership. A professed faith and a consistent Christian life constitute the moral qualifications. And baptism constitutes the ritual or ceremonial qualification.

In that symbolic act one declares oneself dead to the world and sin, buried, and raised up to newness of life through the death and resurrection of Jesus Christ from the dead. The spiritual change of the new birth begets *Christian* fellowship; but to secure *church* fellowship, that change must be confessed in baptism. This is the New Testament order. At the first it was so; they repented, they believed, they were baptized, then added to the church. Without confession in baptism there could be no Christian churches.

4. *A Christian Life*

This condition is obvious. An external Christian life must demonstrate the profession of an internal Christian faith. "If ye then be risen with Christ, seek those things which are above, where Christ sitteth on the right hand of God. Set your affections on things above, not on things on the earth. For ye are dead, and your life is hid with Christ in God" (Col. 3:1-3). No amount of attestation can make the world believe that a person is a Christian whose deeds are not in harmony with his words.

NOTE 1.—Not every person can give an equally satisfactory relation of Christian experience before the church, nor are those always the most certainly regenerate who can tell the most remarkable experience. But no person can consistently be admitted to its fellowship unless the church in some way obtains satisfactory evidence of his conversion.

NOTE 2.—Persons on entering a church may be ignorant of many things in Christian doctrine, and must be ignorant of many things in practical Christian life, which they will afterward learn. They should not be rejected simply on that account. Indeed, they enter the church as a school of sacred learning, to be instructed.

NOTE 3.—In all matters fundamental, both as to faith and practice, members of the same church should hold and act alike, since harmony in the body is of the greatest importance. But it would be unreasonable to demand or expect that considerable numbers of persons, differing in education, habits of thought, constitution of mind, and independent opinions, could attain perfect uniformity of belief in all matters of Christian truth. This would be impracticable, and in minor matters large Christian liberty should be allowed.

NOTE 4.—The relation of Christian experience by the candidate, while the practice should be maintained, cannot usually give full and satisfactory evidence of conversion. The excitement of the occasion and the timidity of the candidate may do injustice to the most devout and pious persons. The pastor, deacons, and others should, by personal inquiry, obtain the facts in the case, and lay them before the body as evidence.

NOTE 5.—Neither age, sex, race, past character, nor condition in life should serve to keep one out of the church, if the evidence be abundant and satisfactory that such a person be truly converted.

B. MODES OF ADMISSION

There are three ways in common use, by which persons may be admitted to the church. Each of these presupposes a vote of the body to receive the candidate. Each new member must be admitted by the free and voluntary consent and approval of those already members, usually expressed by a formal vote. By this method alone, and not by the personal action of the minister, nor yet by the decision of a board or committee, are new members to be received.

The following are the three modes of admission:

1. *By Baptism.*—A person may be admitted to the church on a profession of faith in Christ, by baptism. First he makes known his desire for baptism and union with the church, to the pastor or brethren. If they, after proper investigation, become satisfied of his readiness for that step, the church considers the question of his reception; and then, if satisfied, votes that he be received as a member, on being baptized.

2. *By Letter.*—Members often remove from the vicinity of the church with which they have united. Then it becomes their duty, and should be their desire, to connect themselves with a church of the same faith near their new home, where they can conveniently work and worship. By the comity of Christian fellowship, and by that courtesy which each church owes to each other, the one of which he is a member gives him a letter of commendation and dismission, by which his membership may be transferred to the other. This letter certifies to his good Christian character and regular standing, and commends him to the confidence of, and membership in, the other church. If satisfied, he is received by a vote of the church, as in the former case—the letter serving as a certificate of character and standing, with permission to unite.

3. *By Experience.*—It sometimes happens that persons who have been baptized, but by some means have lost their membership, desire to unite with a church. They bring no letters, nor are they rebaptized; but give an account of their conversion and Christian life. They then are received by vote on their confession.

NOTE 1.—In most churches, all applicants for membership must first go before the board of deacons, and if that board regards the application unfavorably, it is not presented to the church at all.

NOTE 2.—At times it may be found expedient to postpone the reception of a candidate for a better acquaintance. Moreover, it is always better to use great deliberation than to proceed with great haste in such a matter.

NOTE 3.—To baptize persons who do not unite with any church is considered bad policy, as subversive of good order and destructive of church organization. They should be approved and received by the body for full fellowship to take effect *when baptized.* Yet there are possible exceptions to this rule where no church exists, or where the persons are baptized to constitute one, or in some other unusual circumstances.

NOTE 4.—It is customary, when members are admitted to the church, whether by baptism, letter, or experience, for the pastor to give them *the hand of fellowship.* This is usually done at the communion service immediately before the elements are distributed. The candidate rises, while the hand is extended with a few words of kindly welcome. The act is fraternal, but not essential; it is designed simply as an expression of the church's welcome. It does not make them members, and adds nothing to their standing, but recognizes them in the presence of the body as newly-received fellow-disciples.

NOTE 5.—The reception of persons by *restoration* is not essentially different from that by experience. Members who have been excluded from fellowship may be received back when the causes which led to the withdrawal of fellowship are removed, and the individual requests restoration. The church, being satisfied with his fitness, votes his reception. The hand of fellowship properly follows in this case, as in the others. Such cases are reported in the records of the clerk as additions by restoration.

C. Modes of Dismission

The church is more than a mere confederation of men and women; it is the body of Christ, where each one is a member in particular. Each one who unites with it does so, presumably, not as a mere matter of convenience or personal caprice, but from a sense of religious obligation. Baptists hold that Christians should not live outside the fold of the Good Shepherd, but within the shelter of this fellowship. Provision is, however, made for a transfer of membership from one church to another.

There are three ways by which the relation of members to a church may be dissolved:

1. *By Letter.*—A member may, on application, receive a letter of commendation and dismission from his church, with which to unite with another of the same faith.

2. *By Exclusion.*—When the church, in the exercise of its lawful authority and discipline, withdraws fellowship from a person proven to be an unworthy member, his connection with the body is dissolved and thenceforth ceases.

3. *By Death.*—The death of members, of course, dissolves the relation, and transfers them from the church on earth to that above.

NOTE 1.—It is customary for the validity of letters to be limited to some specified time—usually six months—after the expiration of which time they are worthless; but may be renewed, if satisfactory reason be given the church for their non-use.

NOTE 2.—The one receiving a letter is still a member and

subject to the authority and discipline of the church granting it, until he has used it by actually connecting himself with another church.

Note 3.—Letters thus given can be revoked for cause, by the church at its discretion, at any time previous to their being used.

Note 4.—When members remove their residence so far as to render worship with their church impracticable, they should take letters, and unite where they go. Their churches should require this of them, if at all practicable. The too common practice of holding membership in one church, and worshiping in another deserves severe reproof.

Note 5.—Persons excluded from one church should not be received into the fellowship of another, except after careful investigation.

CHAPTER III

THE CHRISTIAN MINISTRY

FEW questions can be so vitally important to any church, whether relating to its own peace and prosperity, or to the success of the work it is appointed to do, as that of the kind of minister who shall serve and lead it. The position commands high regard, for the minister is looked upon not only as a teacher, but as an example. He is therefore accepted as the one who, by his private and public life, is to illustrate the doctrines and ethics which he preaches from the pulpit.

The old prophet's declaration, "like people, like priest," is as true now as when Hosea uttered it. Where the people have freedom of choice, and select their own pastors, they will choose them on the level of their own religious thinking and acting. Moreover, there is a constant tendency on the part of the preacher to keep somewhere near the standard of the people. It requires a heroic effort for the pulpit to rise far above the level of the pew, as to Christian teaching and consecration, and he who long sustains himself in that position may expect, sooner or later, to hear the mutterings of discontent. But then, contradictory as it may seem to be, the converse of the prophet's epigram is equally true: "like priest, like people." For, to a large extent, by faithful, judicious, and persistent endeavor, a godly pastor can mold and win the church to a higher standard.

The old prophets—notably Jeremiah—represented the people of Israel under the analogy of a flock, led and fed and guarded by shepherds, called pastors. Jesus used the same figure when he declared himself to be the Good Shepherd that gave his life for the sheep. The relationship between pastor and people is thus intimate, vital, and sacred.

It is one of the first and most important fruits of religious liberty and free-church polity that congregations of Christian worshipers can elect their own religious teachers. They may make mistakes, but they insist on the right, and they will not willingly submit to the dictation or control of others in this regard, from either civil or ecclesiastical authority. This is a point Baptists have always emphasized, maintaining this as well as other expressions of religious freedom for the individual church. Every Christian is under obligation to preach the gospel according to his ability and opportunity; but special leaders and teachers are needed for the pastorates of churches. The Spirit of God prepares certain men for the work, while the providence of God develops and calls forth their ministry. It is all under the direction of the Chief Shepherd and Bishop of Souls, who sends among his people the under-shepherds.

Jesus began this work while among men. He "ordained twelve, that they should be with him, and that he might send them forth to preach" (Mark 3:14). Likewise, "After these things, the Lord appointed other seventy also, and sent them two and two before his face into every city and place, whither he himself would come" (Luke 10:1). And his final instructions, as he was leaving them, were: "Go ye, therefore, and teach all nations, baptizing them in the name of the Father and of the Son and of the Holy Ghost; teaching them to observe all things whatsoever I have commanded you: and lo, I am with you alway, even unto the end of the world. Amen" (Matt. 28:19, 20).

A. The Purpose of the Ministry

The general purpose contemplated by the appointment and sustenance of an official ministry in the churches is clearly enough defined in the popular mind, and well enough understood by the prevailing customs of religious society: to shepherd the flock, to instruct congregations in religious truth, and to guide the churches as to internal order and the practical activities of Christian life. But, to be more specific, it may be said the ministerial purpose is twofold: the conversion of men, and then their instruction and upbuilding in the faith of the gospel. Thus did Jesus, in his farewell injunction, command his disciples to go forth, preach the gospel, disciple men, baptize them, and then teach them to observe all things whatsoever he had commanded them.

Not infrequently extremists are heard to say that there is nothing comparable to the conversion of souls; that is *the* one great object of preaching. Both goals, however, should be constantly sought, and devotion to one does not exclude the other. God may be as much glorified and the world as much blessed by the development of character and the increase of good works on the part of believers, as by the addition of converts. Read the epistles to the churches, and see how much is said about edifying the body of Christ; about growth in grace; about perfecting the saints in holiness; about being filled with the Spirit.

In Paul's Epistle to the Ephesians, after saying that Christ gave gifts, some to be apostles, prophets, evangelists, pastors, and teachers, he states for what purpose these gifts were bestowed, namely, "For the perfecting of the saints, for the work of the ministry, for the edifying of the body of Christ: till we all come in the unity of the faith, and of the knowledge of the Son of God, unto a perfect man, unto the measure of the stature of the fulness of Christ" (Eph. 4:12, 13). Here is a grand concept of an advancing Christian growth, under the culture of pastors and teachers, even to the attainment of a "perfect man," that is, a perfected humanity in Christ!

When Christians are living in the fullness of the blessing of the gospel and exhibiting the life of Christ, sinners will be converted.

B. THE CALL TO THE MINISTRY

If the spiritual life of the churches is to be maintained, and the power of godliness to be preserved, a *divine call* to the work of the ministry must be insisted on by the churches.

It is not enough that a man—young or old—has piety and ability and education; that he possesses a facility in the use of language, and can address a congregation with ease and interest, both to himself and to them. Nor is it enough that he has an earnest desire to do good. It must not be the mere choice of a profession, nor the dictate of an ambition which looks to the pulpit as a desirable arena for achieving distinction, nor even as the best field for usefulness. Nor must it be a yielding to the opinions or persuasions of overpartial, but, it may be, injudicious friends. A true *call* to the work of the ministry must rest on more solid ground than any or all of these evidences.

"No man taketh this honor unto himself; but he that is called of God, as was Aaron" (Heb. 5:4). He that would enter upon this work must do it from a deep, abiding, and unalterable conviction, wrought into his soul by the Holy Spirit, that such is the will of God concerning him; and that nothing else is, or can be, the work of his life, whether it may bring joy or sorrow, prosperity or adversity. This inward movement and guidance of the Spirit is not always continuous, but recurs from time to time, calling him back from all other purposes and plans to this conviction of duty.

As this conviction is slowly working its way into the soul, various emotions are excited. Not infrequently his mind revolts against what seems the inevitable conclusion. He is troubled by thoughts of unfitness for the work, by the apparent impossibility of being able to secure the proper qualifications, by the fact that many cherished plans for life, which seem to promise more of pleasure and of profit, must be abandoned, and by many other worries. But through it all the Spirit holds his mind true to its destiny, until at length it submits, silences every objection, sacrifices every consideration, accepts every condition, and implicitly obeys the divine call.

The evidences of this divine call are various. The most convincing is that just named, where the Spirit works the ever-deepening conviction into the soul, that it must be so. Another sign is that the mind is being led into a fruitful contemplation of the Scriptures, whose spirit and meaning, whose deep and rich treasures of truth are unfolded and made plain to an unusual degree. Still more, if one has been divinely called to this work, there will soon rise a conviction of the fact in the minds of others. And further: If one is divinely called to preach the gospel, Providence will open ways of preparation for the work. Precisely what that fitting preparation may be, it is impossible here to tell. It should be the best that can be secured.[1]

C. THE SOURCE OF MINISTERIAL AUTHORITY

Whence does the minister derive his authority for the exercise of ministerial functions? Not from the

[1] The American Baptist Convention by resolution at Portland, Oregon, in 1961 defined the educational standard for ordination to the ministry as "including graduation from a recognized college and seminary."

church, for no church holds in itself any such authority to bestow. Not from a council, since councils
possess no ecclesiastical authority. Not from the state,
for the state has no right of interference in matters
of faith and conscience, and possesses no control over
ecclesiastical affairs. The minister, therefore, derives
his credentials from no human source, but directly
from Christ, the great head of the church, by the
witness and endowment which he has received from
the Holy Spirit.

All that a church or a council can properly do is
to recognize and express approval of a man's entering the ministry. The force of ordination is simply a
recognition and sanction, in a public and impressive
manner, of what is believed to be the divine appointment of the candidate to the sacred office. The object
of church and council action is not to impart either
ability or authority to preach the gospel, for these
they cannot give; but to ascertain whether such ability and authority have been divinely given, and if so,
to approve their public exercise.

D. Qualifications for the Ministry

It is not to be expected that of all men the minister
alone will be perfect. And yet in no other man is a
near approach to perfection so imperative as in him.
Of all men, he should prayerfully strive with God's
help to have as few faults and as many excellencies
as possible. For in no other man do they count for so
much, either for or against truth and righteousness,
as in him.

He should be a man of good physical health. This counts for vastly more, even in a spiritual point of view, than is usually supposed. If he is not physically fit, he should, by careful self-training in regard to diet, exercise, and otherwise, strive for improvement. It must not, however, be understood as saying that a man manifestly called of God to the work, should not undertake it because he does not enjoy robust health. Some of the most godly and useful ministers who have ever blessed the world and the churches, have not been vigorous.

Moreover, the minister should be a Christian gentleman in the best sense of that term, courteous, considerate, gentle, generous, and kind to all. There is no excuse for a minister's being rude, boorish, and indifferent to the feelings or comfort of others.

But those special qualifications named by the Apostle, and detailed in the epistles to Timothy and Titus (1 Tim., chap. 3; Titus, chap. 1), should be insisted on by both churches and ordaining councils. According to these inspired specifications, the bishop or pastor should be "blameless, the husband of one wife, vigilant, sober, of good behavior, given to hospitality, apt to teach, not given to wine, no striker, not greedy of filthy lucre, but patient, not a brawler, not covetous, one that ruleth well his own house" (1 Tim. 3:2-4).

E. THE LICENSING OF MINISTERS

It is one of the prevailing customs of our churches to grant a *license* to young men believing themselves, and believed by others, to have been called to preach the gospel, but not yet prepared to enter upon the work of the ministry.[2] This is simply an approval by the church of the course which the candidate is pursuing. It confers no rights and imparts no authority, but expresses the conviction that the bearer possesses gifts and capabilities which indicate a call to the ministry, and a promise of usefulness in it. The giving of licenses is not universal in such cases. Theological schools sometimes require them of students entering, as an evidence that they have the approval and confidence of their churches. Churches should be very careful not to grant licenses without sufficient evidence of a divine call, and not till they have had sufficient opportunity to judge wisely in the case. And where there is good indication of a call, the church should be ready to encourage the candidate in his chosen course, offering him every possible evidence of this support.

F. The Ordination of Ministers

The importance of selecting and placing over the churches the right kind of men as pastors and teachers cannot be overestimated. But the high regard, the almost sanctity, in which our churches hold the *ceremony* of setting apart, of the inauguration of the clergy, finds no parallel and no sanction in the New Testament. The New Testament meaning of the word "ordination" is choosing, electing, appointing a man to the office of bishop or pastor, and has

---

[2] Suitable certificates are sold by most Baptist bookstores.

no reference to a ceremonial setting apart, or investiture with the functions of the office. Our churches, unfortunately, have come to apply the term "ordination" exclusively to the ceremonial induction, and not to the election, which was its primitive and is its proper meaning. No reasonable objection can be made to our usual forms of ordination service, however, providing these forms are rightly understood and held at their right value.

1. *The Election*

The usual course of proceedings in ordinations is as follows:

The church which calls for the ordination—and of which church the candidate should be a member—invites a council, by sending letters to such other churches (and individuals) as it may desire to have present,[3] requesting them to send their pastor and brethren (usually two) to consider and advise them as to the propriety of setting apart the candidate to the work of the gospel ministry.

The council, when convened and organized, listens to a statement from the church calling them, through a committee appointed for the purpose, and then proceeds to the examination of the candidate. This examination usually traverses three principal lines of inquiry, but may go beyond them:

1. His Christian experience.
2. His call to the ministry.

[3] The council, in current practice, is composed of representatives from the churches in the association with which the church is in fellowship. Some associations have provision for a permanent council or advisory committee on ordination.

3. His views of Christian doctrine.

Other topics than these may appropriately be made subjects for inquiry, providing they are germane to the occasion, but remote subjects and profitless discussion should be avoided; especially such subjects as those on which members of the council themselves may be divided.

When the council is satisfied with the examination, the candidate is allowed to retire, while the body proceeds to discuss the matter, and to take action. If there is any serious dissatisfaction, the specific points are considered carefully; and, if desired, the candidate can be recalled to give his views more fully on them. If not, on motion duly made, the council votes its satisfaction on each of the above three distinct topics of inquiry. Then a final vote to this effect is passed: "*Resolved:* that being satisfied with the result of our examination, we approve the setting apart of the candidate, and recommend that the church proceed to the public services of ordination." As the council was called to *advise* the church, this is the advice they give. A committee is then designated, of which the candidate and the representatives of his church are the essential members, to plan the ceremony.

2. *The Ceremony*

What the various parts of the ordination service shall be, and who shall perform them, is optional according to the wishes of the candidate and the church. Usually they are as follows:

1. Opening hymn, invocation, and reading of the Scriptures.

2. Sermon, preached usually by some one previously selected by the candidate.

3. A charge to the candidate, an address, usually by some older minister, reminding him of the various duties and responsibilities the ministry imposes.

4. A charge to the church, an address enjoining on the members their reciprocal duties and responsibilities, in consequence of his settlement among them; duties to him, to themselves, and to the community.

5. The ordaining prayer, during which the candidate kneels. Near the close of this, he who offers the prayer, and some others, lay their hands on the candidate's head.

6. The hand of fellowship, a short address welcoming the candidate to the fellowship and fraternity of the ministry, and to all the pleasures and toils of the sacred service. A certificate of ordination may be presented at this time (or, if this is not convenient, it should be given at a later date).

7. The benediction, usually pronounced by the candidate.

3. *Reordination*

The question of reordination arises when a minister of some other denomination unites with us, and wishes to become a pastor among us. He has professed conformity to our denominational views, and has been baptized into our fellowship. But that gives him only the standing of a private member and not that of a minister. He was, however, an accredited minister in an evangelical denomination before, regularly set apart to the sacred office. Now, the question is, in order to become a Baptist minister, will his previous ordination suffice, or should he be ordained again as though he had never been a clergyman? On this point opinions somewhat differ. Some answer in the affirmative and some in the negative. But really it makes very little difference which course is pursued. Either would be *valid*, and neither is *essential*.

G. The Pastoral Office

In the New Testament the term *episcopos*, which is usually rendered *bishop*, and *presbuteros*, which is rendered *elder*, are used interchangeably, and often applied to the same person. The *episcopos* was an *overseer*, as the term properly denotes; it was the word used chiefly by the Greek Christians as applied to the *pastor*, who had the oversight of the flock, and performed the work of a shepherd in spiritual concerns. The term *presbuteros* or *elder*, was evidently derived from the synagogue, and used chiefly by Jewish Christians to designate the same person.

The term *pastor* signifies a shepherd, and well indicates the nature of the relation he sustains to the church; that of leading, feeding, guiding, and guarding the flock committed to his care. He is also called a *minister* (*diakonos*), one who serves and ministers to others.

The *pastorate* and the *ministry* are related, but not identical. A pastor is a minister, but a minister is not necessarily a pastor. The minister is the *kerux*, the herald, who preaches the gospel, who proclaims the glad tidings to men. The pastor is the *poimen*, who feeds and leads and cares for the flock. The pastor has the care of a church; the minister is a preacher, and may or may not have the care of a church. James is understood to have been pastor of the church in Jerusalem; but Paul and Barnabas, Apollos and Cephas preached the gospel from place to place, as ambassadors of Christ and heralds of the great salvation, planting churches and setting in order affairs, but without a local and permanent pastorate.

1. *Nature of the Pastor's Work*

The religious cultivation of his church and congregation constitutes the particular work of the pastor. It is the shepherding of the flock. He is not to be indifferent to their temporal interests, but their spiritual welfare is his special charge. He is to be the ever-ready, sympathizing and helpful friend to all; but his endeavors should aim at, and be made subservient to, the purpose of the gospel—to win souls to Christ, and guide the people in Christian growth.

The *pulpit* will constitute the stronghold of his ministry to his congregation and the community. Though a pastor, he must still be a preacher to his flock. While some men have not, and cannot have the same attractive power in the pulpit as others, yet sound gospel sermons, ably prepared and earnestly delivered, constitute the only kind of pulpit service which can long commend itself to the consciences of the people. He who neglects his pulpit preparation, for any cause whatever, will find frequent pastoral changes to be imperative—and possibly not always in the most pleasant way.

Emphasis must also be laid on *pastoral visitation.* Here especially he is the pastor. He may not visit so much as many would wish, to be sure, nor should he visit to the detriment of his pulpit preparation. However, he must know his people in their homes; must know their joys and sorrows as they themselves will relate them. They must know him, as they cannot know him in the pulpit simply. Both he and they miss boundless good, if this be not done.

The pastor has the oversight and *supervision* of all the interests of the church, and of all departments of its work, both spiritual and temporal. He should not needlessly interfere with the deacons, or trustees, or Christian education workers, nor assume dictatorial authority over others. Yet it is his privilege and his duty to hold a watchful supervision over all the work of the church, that the purposes of Christ may be served in every way possible.

The pastor should be concerned for the religious nurture of children and youth, but not to the neglect of others. Adult education and the care of the elderly are also important parts of his responsibility. Likewise, class distinctions should never be encouraged or countenanced. He is equally the shepherd of all his flock.

2. *How Pastors Are Obtained*

Churches secure their pastors by election, as the free choice of the people, in each individual church. It is an essential part of the independence of the churches, the right to choose their pastors and teachers. No individual or combination of men can appoint pastors over them, nor compel a church to accept as officers those whom they have not chosen. This is the polity of the New Testament, and has ever been the usage of our people. A free people demand and maintain the right to choose their own rulers. They may ask or accept advice, but no man is a pastor to any people until he has been chosen by their majority vote.

The selection and election of a pastor is one of the most important acts—if not the most important—pertaining to the independence of the church. The interest of the body, and the welfare of religion depend so largely on it, that it should be entered upon with the utmost care, deliberation, and prayer for divine direction.

A pulpit committee is appointed by the church as its representatives to examine credentials, interview, and hear the preaching of persons whose names have been suggested for the pastorate. When satisfied that God has led them to the man of his choosing for the position, the committee arranges a suitable occasion for presenting him to the church, when he will preach at a regular service and meet the people personally. Shortly thereafter a business meeting of the church is held, and a vote is taken as to whether to extend a call to him.[4]

When the choice is made and the pastor secured, then let him be received, loved, supported, honored, and obeyed, as one sent of God for this sacred work. And let it be further considered that no man can do

[4] The pulpit committee has evolved since the time of the author, and this paragraph, therefore, is added by the present editors.

of himself all that is desired and expected of a pastor. He must not only have divine help, but he must have the sympathy, cooperation, and prayers of the church. Some miserable failures in the ministry are due to the faults of the ministers themselves; still more are due to the churches, which too often are unkind toward the pastor whom they had professed to be chosen of God.

3. *The Pastor's Authority*

The pastor is placed over the church by both the appointment of God and the free and voluntary act of the church itself. On the one hand, he is not to be regarded with ignorant and blind devotion, as if possessed of superhuman attributes, nor yet, on the other hand, is he to be considered a mere puppet.

As a rule, the pastor who maintains a dignified and consistent Christian and ministerial life, commending himself to the confidence of the people, will receive all the deference he desires, and will have accorded to him all that personal respect and official reverence which he needs to claim. His authority will be a moral force, to which those who love and honor him will yield. He need not worry and fret because he does not receive the respect which he thinks his due. Let him command it by his character and deportment. He may attempt too much to enforce his authority. As a preacher of the gospel his authority is of another and a higher kind, in that he is an ambassador from the King, and speaks with an authority more than human. True, his words, even in the pulpit, are not beyond question, since they are to be judged by the infallible standard of the Word of God. But in the administration of church affairs he should secure the cooperation of his members, and gain his object by reason and persuasion, rather than attempting to force compliance by authoritative dictation.

4. *Length of Pastorate*

It is unquestionably true that long pastorates have their trials no less severe—sometimes more painful—than short ones. The pastor has more than once seen the time when, restless and uneasy, he would gladly have resigned, had any eligible field elsewhere opened for him. And the church has more than once seen the time when it would have rejoiced at a change, but had too much regard for him, and too much respect for themselves, to force a change. Many a pastor, who has the faculty of "holding on," has outlived his usefulness on a given field, either because devoted to the theory of long pastorates or because he saw no way to better his situation; and that, too, very likely, when he knew the people would be quite willing for a change for the sake of the cause, though they loved and honored him.

Quite as unfortunate in its effects, and more frequently than long and fruitless pastorates, is the sudden and hasty change so often made by many, and sometimes on the most trivial occasion. There are in every church, most likely, mischief-makers, whose influence is chiefly felt in opposing others and stirring up strife. Let a pastor possess his soul in patience, and not be made unhappy by every little cross-current in his affairs. But if any considerable number of his kind, prudent, and judicious brethren think a change is desirable; or if he himself, after long and prayerful consideration, believes it his duty to leave, let him act accordingly. But let a minister flee "church quarrels" as he would a pestilence. He may not be responsible for them, but if he becomes involved in them, though the merits of the case may be on his side, yet he cannot remain to fight them out without suffering more in peace of mind and reputation than any victory he can win will be worth. Let him retire to other fields, where he can serve without conflict, and leave the fighting to those who have less at stake. The world is wide, and he can do good and be happy in many another field.

5. *Pastoral Support*

A pastor should be well and generously supported as to his salary, according to the ability of the church he serves. He will not expect to live up to the standard of the wealthiest; he ought not to be expected to live down to the standard of the poorest.

When the church extends a call, they name the amount they are willing to pay. Of course it is optional with him whether to accept the call on such conditions. If he does, he cannot find fault that they give no more—unless, indeed, as is not infrequently the case, they delude him with the promise that they will increase the amount the next year; a promise often made, but not always kept. But let the stipulated sum be regularly and promptly paid, otherwise he will not be able promptly to pay his debts, and his reputation will be compromised and his character imperiled. It is a bad thing for a clergyman to get the name of not paying his debts.

6. *The Pastor a Peacemaker*

Troubles in church life unfortunately sometimes arise. And whether the pastor be the cause or only the victim of them, he always more or less suffers from them. Very many of these troubles are no doubt to be charged upon pastors themselves. A minister of the gospel, of all men, should be a peacemaker. He should soothe and heal. It is better for himself and better for all concerned. He must "endure hardness as a good soldier of Jesus Christ." Of course he has his rights, which are not to be lightly invaded, but he is to be an example to the flock in patient endurance.

On the other hand, the church should carefully guard the reputation and the feelings of their pastor, and not allow the gossip-loving or the envious to assail him. His people are bound to protect him. If he be in fault, let them tell him so, and win him from his mistakes.

Both pastor and people should regard all dissension and strife with so much dread as to check it by any amount of effort and sacrifice at the very beginning. Churches cannot be expected to prosper, or the gospel to have free course, while rent by dissension and strife, especially by strife connected with, or on account of the pastor. The philosophy of spiritual and religious growth is the same now as when this record was made: "Then had the churches rest throughout all Judea and Galilee and Samaria, and were edified; and walking in the fear of the Lord, and in the comfort of the Holy Ghost, were multiplied" (Acts 9:31).

NOTE 1.—In calling a man to the pastorate, the church should take deliberate care to know his record; what he has done elsewhere, and how he is esteemed and valued where he has previously lived and labored. It is a folly of which churches are often guilty—and for which they justly suffer— that on the credit of a few flashy or fascinating sermons, wholly ignorant of his private character and of his ministerial history, they call and settle a pastor. A man of deep Christian commitment, thoroughly in love with the word of God, is much to be preferred to the brilliant pulpiteer.

NOTE 2.—If a young man without a record is called to be ordained and begin his pastorate, his reputation for commitment, sound sense, and pulpit ability should be carefully considered and well understood. If he be of the right spirit and the right material, he will grow into larger usefulness through study, the endowment of the Spirit, and the prayers of the people.

NOTE 3.—In giving a *call*, the church usually appoints a meeting for that express purpose, notice being publicly given two Sundays in succession, the purpose of the meeting being distinctly stated in the notice, and a three-quarters vote of all present at such a meeting should be deemed essential to a call. Certainly no self-respecting man would accept a call on anything less than that. Such meeting should be managed with Christian sincerity, and the candidate should be informed exactly how the vote stands, and what the feeling toward him is, concealing nothing.

H. ACCUSED MINISTERS

One of the most grave and difficult cases of discipline which is likely to arise to vex and possibly to divide a church is that of a minister who has lost public confidence, and who, by unchristian or unministerial conduct, is believed to be unfit to discharge the functions of, or to remain in, the sacred office.

Great caution should be exercised, even in giving heed to unfavorable reports against a minister of the gospel. The Apostle wisely decreed, "Against an elder, receive not an accusation but before two or three witnesses" (1 Tim. 5:19). Charges which implicate their moral or ministerial character should not be entertained, except on very strong evidence. Their position is a very delicate one. Called by professional duties into almost all sorts of company, and placed in well-nigh all kinds of positions, they can become the victims of suspicions aroused by evil-minded persons against them on the most trivial occasions. They themselves are bound to exercise perpetual vigilance and care, while their reputation and good character, on which their comfort and usefulness so much depend, should be sacredly guarded and defended. But their sins should not be covered when they deserve exposure, nor should they escape discipline when they merit it.

Such cases are likely to be important and difficult, because:

First—Of the high position and wide influence of a minister, and the fact that he stands before the public as an example of godliness, a religious teacher and leader of the people. If he proves himself an unworthy man, his case becomes more a reproach to religion, and more an obstacle to the progress of truth than if he were a private member of the church.

Second—A minister's character and good name must be held sacredly and dealt with tenderly, since they are his richest possessions. They must not be trifled with.

In dealing with such a case, therefore, unusual caution should be exercised; and there are few churches so strong, so wise, so well balanced and so self-contained that it would be prudent to proceed to extremities without in some way securing outside aid and advice, most likely through the association or the state convention. In many instances, with such guidance, deacons or other officers of the church can bring the matter to a satisfactory solution by private conference with the pastor.

In the most extreme situations, a council similar to an ordination council may be convened to review the case and make suitable recommendations. Such a council may suggest, after hearing both the accusations and the defense, some disciplinary action, or may vote that he has been wronged and should be cleared of all charges.

A council called to advise in matters relating to the trial of an accused minister can only be called by a church; and by that church of which such minister is a member. Having no ecclesiastical authority, it cannot be called to try, nor if he is found guilty, to depose a minister. Judicial acts belong to a church, and not to a council; nor can a church transfer its authority for the exercise of judicial functions to any other body. A council, in order to express an opinion and give advice, is asked to examine all the facts, consider all the circumstances, sift and weigh the evidence on all sides, the accused having full opportunity to defend himself. In a modified, but not in a judicial sense, it may be called a trial of the accused, because it is a search for the merits of the case by an investigation of all the facts and a sifting of all the evidence.

The minister on whose case his church may call a council is not obliged, and cannot be compelled, to appear before such a council, or in any way submit his case to them. But it is his *right* to appear before them, have copies of all charges, hear all testimony, examine witnesses, and answer for himself, and usually it is better for him to take this course. It is better for one to meet all charges frankly, and all accusers face to face, than to seem to evade an investigation of matters laid against him.

The final action of a church, as to an accused minister, may take any one of the following forms:

1. That of an *acquittal*, where no fault worthy of further consideration was proven against him; the charges were not sustained, and he is pronounced innocent.

2. That of *admonition:* To caution and admonish him to greater circumspection may be all which the case requires.

3. That of a *withdrawal of fellowship from him as a minister of the gospel*, with a declaration that in their opinion he is unworthy of, and unfit to continue in, the ministerial office. This may be done, and the man still be retained in the fellowship of the church as a private member. There may be faults

which would disqualify him for the exercise of a public ministry, but might not unfit him for private membership. Such an act of disfellowship as a minister would virtually be an act of deposition from the sacred office, so far as any act of church or council could depose him.

4. That of the *withdrawal of fellowship from him as a church member*, thus excluding him from the body. This, accompanied with a declaration of his unworthiness as a minister of the gospel, constitutes the final and utmost act of the church's disciplinary power, in such a case. They can do no more. This puts him out, and deposes him from the ministry, so far as any human power can depose him. It also clears the church from any further responsibility as to his character or conduct. His disfellowship as a *member* adds emphasis to his disfellowship as a *minister*.

To the above-named acts a council may advise; but the acts themselves, to be valid and of any force, must be the acts of the church and not of the council. It would be an impertinent assumption for a council to attempt such an exercise of ecclesiastical authority.

CHAPTER IV

CHURCH OFFICERS

WHAT are the officers of a Baptist church? How are they secured? What are their functions? And whence is their authority? These are questions of importance to be asked and answered; and to which various replies will be given. But suppose we first make the questions somewhat more specific, and ask, "What are the scriptural officers of a church?" We shall by this means simplify the inquiry, and be directed to the New Testament for an answer.

In the New Testament we find that in apostolic times, and for many years after, pastors and deacons only were known as permanent church officers. Others have been added at later times, for a variety of reasons.

We have considered the ministry in all its aspects, including the pastoral office, in the preceding chapter. The sections which follow, therefore, will be devoted to the work of the laity as church officers—first to the diaconate, the lone non-pastoral office found in the New Testament, and then to the other offices which have been added to meet the changing needs of the churches.

A. Deacons

The term *deacon* (*diakonos*) in the New Testament means literally a minister, a servant, one who ministers to, or serves others. This, taken in a large sense, gives a very wide range of meaning to the word. It is applied to the Apostles and even to Christ himself. In ecclesiastical usage, however, it designates an officer in the church.

1. *Their Origin*

The diaconate is usually supposed to have originated in the election of the Seven, as helpers to the Apostles, recorded in Acts 6:1-6, though they were not called *deacons*. Subsequent to Pentecost, the large ingathering of converts had so multiplied the number that the care of the needy became a burden to the Apostles, so great as seriously to interfere with their spiritual duties in the ministry of the word. Hence, having called the multitude of the disciples together, they explained the matter and requested them to select "seven men of honest report, full of the Holy Ghost, and wisdom," to whom this service should be committed, that they themselves might give themselves "continually to prayer and to the ministry of the word." This request was complied with and seven men selected, whom the Apostles set apart to the work for which they were chosen, by prayer and the laying-on of hands.

2. *Their Duties*

Deacons are to be chosen by a free vote of the church, and are to be faithful, prudent, experienced, and devout men. They are to have charge of the sick and needy members, and are also to act as counselors and assistants to the pastor in advancing the general interests of the body. In the absence of a pastor it becomes the duty of the deacons to conduct the devotional meetings, provide for the supply of the pulpit and administer the affairs of the body generally. Of the original seven, Philip and Stephen were most effective preachers of the gospel, but it was not for this that they were especially chosen. With many of our churches the deaconship has come to be a merely nominal affair, regarded as of small importance, and accomplishing a questionable service. This ought not to be so.

3. *Their Number*

The number of deacons in a church is a matter discretionary with the body, varying according to the size of the church. Some authorities suggest that there be one deacon for every 25 to 50 members, with a minimum of two in the smallest churches.

4. *Their Time of Service*

The period of time for which they are chosen, as well as the number, is discretionary with the church, since no scriptural precept or precedent directs. The practice of electing them for a limited period has come to be quite prevalent, generally for three years. In this way the office expires by limitation, and if better men are available they can be chosen without offense. In many churches, to encourage this freedom of choice, it is provided that a deacon who has served two terms in succession may not be elected to another until a year's time has elapsed.

5. *Their Ordination*

The Seven were set apart to the discharge of their duties by prayer and the laying-on of hands by the Apostles, as indicating the sacred and important duties committed to them. In our older churches this practice was carefully adhered to, but it has fallen very much into disuse. Ordination, if generally practiced, would invest the office with more importance. Too much care cannot be taken to secure the right kind of men, when we consider that the permanent influence of a deacon is scarcely surpassed by that of the pastor himself. A good deacon is a blessing both to the pastor and the church.

NOTE 1.—It is evident from the character of the Seven, and the personal history of some of them subsequently, that while their specific official duties were the temporalities of the church, yet at the same time they were foremost as counselors and coadjutors with the Apostles in the spiritual interests as well. Having been among the most devout, prudent, and faithful before their election, and as the reason for their election, they would not be less so afterward. Such are the men for the office.

NOTE 2.—Some people and some churches seem to think, that about the only duty of a deacon is to pass the elements at the celebration of the Lord's Supper. And so the office becomes almost a nullity. Anyone on whom the pastor may call can pass the elements. The original "serving of tables" was quite a different work from this. The diaconate implies a substantial and an important service in the church, of which the serving at the Supper is a proper (but only an incidental) adjunct. If their practical relations to the church be reduced to this, they may well be considered as little more than an ornamental appendage to an organization.

Note 3.—The secular concerns of the church, including its financial affairs, would seem legitimately to be embraced in the duties of the deaconship according to the original purpose, as belonging to its temporalities, but now these matters are usually committed to an entirely different class of men known as trustees, elected under the specific direction of State laws.

Note 4.—Deacons should be watchful guardians of the purity and good order of the churches, striving to maintain a healthful tone of Christian faith and activity in the body. But they must act only in conjunction with the pastor, not independent of him, except possibly in very rare and urgent cases. Hence, while it is desirable for the pastor to have meetings with his deacons often or statedly for consultation and advice, it is not proper for them to hold meetings as a board of deacons, independent of and without the advice of the pastor.

Note 5.—Some churches have the practice of electing deaconesses to minister to the sick and to perform other services to those of their own sex. It is difficult to see why such a class of helpers, more or less formally designated for Christian work, should not be continued in our churches. They may serve either as a separate board or as fellow members of the board of deacons.

B. Other Officers[1]

In addition to those church officers described in the New Testament, others have become necessary

---

[1] This section has been rewritten since the time of Dr. Hiscox to provide information on more recent trends and customs with regard to church officers.

as church life in modern times has become more complex. Whereas at one time the board of deacons was the only church board, most churches now have a board of trustees, and many have a board of Christian education. Some have a board of deaconesses as a separate entity, although this function is often combined with that of the deacons, with both men and women as members. There are also those churches which have a board of missions and/or a board of ushers, but many prefer committee status for these functions.

Individual officers found in many churches include the clerk, the treasurer, the financial secretary, the moderator, and the church school superintendent, all of whom are generally selected from the lay membership of the church. It is also common to employ various staff members to work with and assist the pastor, such as an associate pastor, director of Christian education, minister of music, church secretary, and sexton, depending upon the size and resources of the church.

Many of the functions of the church are also administered or cared for through committees, such as the nominating committee, music committee, ushering committee, auditing committee, communications committee, committee on Christian social concern, evangelism committee, committee on world mission support, and finance committee.

Detailed discussion of all of these officers is not possible within the compass of this book, but the following paragraphs will provide a general guide, and may be supplemented by reference to other books such as *A Baptist Manual of Polity and Practice,* by Norman H. Maring and Winthrop S. Hudson and *Church Officers at Work,* by Glenn H. Asquith.

1. *The Board of Trustees*

State laws relating to religious corporations, as a rule, require that there be a specific body which holds legal title to the property of the church and is responsible for its financial affairs. In fact, the law sometimes even spells out the number, tenure, and method of election of the members of such a body. Usually this is the board of trustees, although in some instances these duties are combined with those of the board of deacons. Trustees are usually responsible for the development of an annual every-member financial canvass and for the administration of the budget. The drafting of the budget, however, is done by some more widely representative group such as the advisory council, and its approval can occur only through action of the church itself. Trustees are usually elected on a rotating basis for three-year terms, so that only one-third of the terms expire each year. Many churches provide that trustees may not be reelected until a year's lapse, after serving two consecutive terms.

2. *The Board of Christian Education*

The entire educational program of the church may well be placed under the jurisdiction of a board elected for this purpose on three-year rotating terms similar to those of the board of trustees. The work of this board may be carried out in part through committees on children's work, youth work, adult work, leadership education, and missionary and stewardship education, whose chairmen comprise the board together with the board chairman. Ex-officio members include the pastor, church school superintendent, evening fellowship coordinator, and director of Christian education.

3. *The Clerk*

The church clerk is an elected officer who is responsible for keeping a complete and accurate record of church business meetings, writing official letters on behalf of the church, and maintaining the membership roll in good order. The member selected for this position is usually one who is meticulously accurate, and it is good that he be reelected many times if he does his work well, in order to profit fully from his accumulated understanding and experience.

4. *The Treasurer*

The church treasurer is an elected officer who works closely with the board of trustees as the custodian of church funds, receiving the members' tithes and contributions from the financial secretary and making payments as authorized by the trustees. It is good business practice for him to be bonded and for his records to be audited annually. Like the clerk, he is an officer whose accumulated experience is of particular value, and it is wise to re-elect several times a treasurer whose work is satisfactory.

5. *The Moderator*

The moderator is that person who is designated to preside over church business meetings and meetings of the advisory council. Some churches automatically designate the pastor as their moderator; others have a lay member elected for the purpose.

6. *The Financial Secretary*

The financial secretary is responsible for the exacting and confidential task of maintaining accurate records as to the financial contributions of the members. If a system of pledging is followed, the financial secretary has a record of the amounts pledged; he identifies the payments as they are received each week through numbered offering envelopes, and records them in his book. At regular intervals, perhaps once a quarter, he sends each contributor a written notice as to the status of his account. An accurate statement sent at the end of the calendar year will prove a useful aid to the contributor in computing his income tax.

7. *The Church School Superintendent*

In earlier years it was common to find a Sunday school, meeting in conjunction with the church, but entirely independent from it and having its own elected officers and its own finances. More recently, the trend has developed by which the Sunday morning school has become an educational activity of the church itself, and therefore it has been called the *Sunday church school.* Under this plan, its superintendent is an officer of the church, elected by the membership of the church; the funds are handled by the church treasurer; and the work as a whole is under the church board of Christian education.

8. *Employed Staff*

Most churches are fortunate enough to have at

least one or two additional staff members other than
the pastor, even if only on a part-time basis. In our
increasingly specialized world, this provides capable
personnel on a somewhat permanent basis for the
more specialized responsibilities of the church. It has
the further advantage of allowing all members of the
church to participate in these phases of the work,
since their contributions to the operating budget provide the salaries. It goes without saying that the
people selected for these positions should be dedicated Christians with definite capabilities in their
fields, and with personality characteristics which will
enable them to work well with others in the church.
They usually serve in relation to some specific board
or committee, but always under the administrative
direction of the pastor. For example, an associate
pastor might be related to the board of deacons, a
director of Christian education to the board of Christian education, a minister of music to the music committee or board of trustees, a church secretary to the
board of deacons, a sexton to the board of trustees.
At the same time, they will welcome the general guidance of the pastor and will keep him informed as to
their work.

9. *Committees*

Committees differ from boards in several ways:
(1) they are less permanent, having terms usually of
one year instead of perhaps three; (2) they have more
sharply defined areas of service and responsibility;
(3) they may be appointive rather than elective; and
(4) their duties are likely to be less strenuous.

Some committees frequently found in Baptist churches are those responsible for ushering, music, Christian social concern, evangelism, flowers, personnel or nominations, mission support, finance, auditing, and communications. These are, of course, in addition to the committees of the various boards and the pulpit committee, which serves only during a pastoral interim.

10. *The Advisory Council*

It is common in many churches to have an advisory council consisting of the elected officers of the church, the chairmen of boards and committees, and the presidents of auxiliary organizations. This council serves as a general overseer of church life, studying long-range plans, coordinating the work of the various groups represented, and working out cooperative programs. It does not make any basic and binding decisions upon the church, but leaves these for the church business meeting. Details are usually assigned to the related boards, committees, and organizations for carrying out.

11. *Church Representatives*

Various community organizations of a Christian nature, such as homes for the aged, children's homes, hospitals, and councils of churches, may request the church to provide representation on their boards of directors or managers. If the church wishes to be so represented, it should choose persons who will take their responsibilities seriously, entering into the work of these institutions with enthusiasm and interest, and keeping the church in touch with what they are doing. These representatives may or may not be designated in the constitution as officers of the church; but, if they are not so designated, their work is usually second only to that of the officers in its significance, and on occasion may take on great importance.

CHAPTER V

CHRISTIAN ORDINANCES

CHRISTIAN ordinances may be defined as "institutions of divine authority relating to the worship of God, under the Christian dispensation." In this general sense there are various ordinances, since preaching and hearing the word, prayer, singing, fasting, and thanksgiving may all be considered as institutions of divine authority.

But in a narrower and a more distinctive sense it has been common to call *baptism* and the *Lord's Supper* by this name, and to say they are the only Christian ordinances committed to the churches, and are for perpetual observance. These rites are also called sacraments by some, but, in the sense in which many ritualistic churches use the term, baptism and the Supper are not sacraments at all. Sacraments are interpreted by them to mean not simply outward signs of inward grace and spiritual operations, but outward rites which work grace and produce spiritual operations. This view is rejected by most Protestants and by Baptists in particular.

These two, therefore, baptism and the Supper, are the only sacred rites enjoined by Christ for perpetual observance in his churches. They are not only visible signs which appeal to the senses, but teaching institutions which appeal to the understanding and the heart. Their claim to respect and observance rests not on their peculiar fitness, though that is manifest, but on the simple fact that Christ has established them and commanded their observance.

A. Baptism[1]

Baptism is sometimes called "the initiatory rite," because persons are not received to membership in the churches until they are baptized. Actually, baptism of itself does not admit to the fellowship of the churches; it, however, stands at the door, and admission is only on its reception. It has by some been called "the seal of the new covenant," as circumcision was the seal of the old. It is, however, a witness and a testimony to the covenant, since it is naturally and properly the first Christian act of the believer after an exercise of saving faith. It certifies therefore to the acceptance of Christ, and the union and fellowship of the renewed soul with its Savior. It becomes a badge of discipleship, and is, in that sense, a seal of the covenant of grace.

1. *Its Institution*

Christian baptism was instituted by Christ when he submitted to John's baptism, adopting its form

---

[1] For a comprehensive treatise on baptism by Dr. Hiscox, see *The Hiscox Guide for Baptist Churches.*

with some change of meaning. John's baptism was unto repentance and faith in him who was to come. Jesus baptized (or his disciples did) into himself, as the Messiah who had come, and as the sign that his kingdom had already been established in the hearts of those who received it.

This baptism did not come in the place of circumcision or any other sign or seal of the old covenant, but was ordained for the new. Thus, "John did baptize in the wilderness, and preach the baptism of repentance for the remission of sins" (Mark 1:4). "John answered, saying unto them all, I indeed baptize you with water, but one mightier than I cometh, the latchet of whose shoes I am not worthy to unloose; he shall baptize you with the Holy Ghost and with fire" (Luke 3:16). "Then cometh Jesus from Galilee to Jordan, unto John, to be baptized of him. And Jesus, when he was baptized, went up straightway out of the water: and, lo, the heavens were opened unto him, and he saw the Spirit of God descending like a dove and lighting upon him: and lo, a voice from heaven saying, This is my beloved Son, in whom I am well pleased" (Matt. 3:13, 16, 17). "Go ye therefore, and teach all nations, baptizing them in the name of the Father, and of the Son, and of the Holy Ghost, teaching them to observe all things whatsoever I have commanded you: and, lo, I am with you alway, even unto the end of the world" (Matt. 28:19, 20).

The circumstances in which this characteristic Christian rite was inaugurated, as well as the personal glory of him who appointed, and who com-

manded it as a badge of discipleship for all who
confess his name, make it impressive in its simple
form, and sacred in its influence on both those who
receive and those who witness it.

2. *Its Administration*

Christian baptism is defined as the immersion of
a person in water, on a profession of his faith in
Christ, in, or into, the name of the Father, Son, and
Holy Spirit. The word comes from the Greek *bap-
tizo*, which means "immerse" or "dip," and therefore
it cannot be applied properly to pouring or sprin-
kling. As used in the New Testament, *baptize* always
implies immersion.

Jesus himself was baptized by immersion in the
Jordan. Of this event it is said, "And Jesus, when he
was baptized, went up straightway out of the water"
(Matt. 3:16). Again, it is recorded that Jesus "was
baptized of John in Jordan; and straightway
coming out of the water, he saw the heavens opened"
(Mark 1:9-10). Does not the very fact of his going
down into the water, so as to come up out of the
water, show presumptively (if not positively) that
his baptism was an immersion, or burial in the water?

Christian practice in New Testament times followed the same custom: "And were baptized of him
in Jordan, confessing their sins" (Matt. 3:6). "And
they went down both into the water, both Philip and
the eunuch, and he baptized him" (Acts 8:38).
"Therefore we are buried with him by baptism into
death" (Rom. 6:4). "Buried with him in baptism"
(Col. 2:12). This impressive form and manner of

administration of baptism by immersion was practiced by Christ and his apostles, and continued unchanged in the churches until the introduction of infant baptism brought changes which destroyed its beauty and robbed it of its significance.

3. *Its Subjects*

Baptism is to be administered to those, and to those only, who have exercised and professed a saving faith in Christ; that is, to *believers*. This saving faith presupposes repentance for sin, and a turning to the Lord with full commitment of heart.

Pedobaptists say baptism is to be given to believers and their *children*. But the New Testament knows nothing of the baptism of infants, nor does it teach that children can be partakers of grace simply because of the faith of their parents. Each one must believe for himself in order that he may be saved. "He that believeth and is baptized shall be saved; but he that believeth not shall be damned" (Mark 16:16). But "when they believed . . . they were baptized, both men and women" (Acts 8:12). "Then they that gladly received his word were baptized" (Acts 2:41). "If thou believest with all thine heart, thou mayest" (Acts 8:37). None but believers were baptized.

If baptism be "an outward sign of an inward grace," then it can have no significance to those who have not received the inward cleansing of the Spirit.

4. *Its Obligation*

All men are under obligation to repent of sin, and to accept Christ as their only means of salvation. And all believers in Christ are bound by the most sacred considerations to obey their Lord's command, and confess him before men in baptism. No one who trusts him for salvation can willingly disregard his command, nor neglect the public profession of faith which this ordinance affords.

It is not a question as to whether he can be saved without baptism, but whether he can be a true disciple, and refuse or neglect thus to obey and confess his Savior. "Repent and be baptized, every one of you, in the name of Jesus Christ" (Acts 2:38). "Arise and be baptized, and wash away thy sins" (Acts 22: 16). Baptism may not be essential to salvation, but it is essential to obedience. The wish to live unrecognized as a Christian, unwilling to share the responsibilities, or to discharge the duties of discipleship, and yet hoping for all its blessings and rewards, is both selfish and mercenary, and indicates that the new birth has not yet transpired.

5. *Its Efficacy*

It may well be asked, What is the efficacy of baptism? What does it do for him who receives it? In what respect is the disciple different, after his baptism, from what he was before? In reply it may be most positively stated that baptism does not produce faith and a new heart. It possesses no magical power to convert the soul. Regeneration is by the Holy Spirit alone, and should precede baptism.

But as an act of obedience to Christ, the reception of this ordinance usually brings light, joy, and comfort to the soul. Moreover, the disciple feels that in baptism he has effectually and openly come out from the world, and committed himself to Christ and his service. This gives triumph to the spirit, and fills it with boundless peace.

Baptism, therefore, is an act of obedience, and as such brings the candidate into a more intimate and exclusive fellowship with his Lord; but it possesses no power in itself to remit sin, to change the heart, or to sanctify the spirit.

6. *Its Significance*

Baptism has its retrospect and its prospect. It points back to Christ in his humiliation, death, burial, and resurrection; and keeps constantly in the minds of both candidates and spectators him who died for our sins and rose again for our justification. It testifies that he suffered, died, was buried, and rose from the dead, to perfect the work of redemption.

What God did in Christ gives to this ordinance its significance and its force. "Buried with him in baptism, wherein also ye are risen with him" (Col. 2:12). The past is brought to view. There is "one Lord, one faith, one baptism" (Eph. 4:5), thus forever connecting the disciple in this act with his Lord. "We are buried with him by baptism, into death: that like as Christ was raised up from the dead by the glory of the Father, even so we also should walk in newness of life" (Rom. 6:4). If the past could be forgotten, this sacred ordinance would lose its moral power.

At the same time, baptism also is predictive. It foreshadows the resurrection of the believer's body from the grave. He rises from the baptismal waters like Christ from the dead.

Baptism is also a confession of faith. The symbolism of that sacred rite teaches the great cardinal doctrines of the gospel, such as:

Christ's death and burial for our sins, and his resurrection from the dead for our justification: "But I have a baptism to be baptized with; and how am I straitened till it be accomplished!" (Luke 12:50).

Death to sin, rising to a new spiritual life in Christ, and fellowship with the Lord, both in dying and living: "For as many of you as have been baptized into Christ have put on Christ" (Gal. 3:27).

The resurrection of the saints, of which the resurrection of Christ is the prophecy and the pledge: "For if we have been planted together in the likeness of his death, we shall be also in the likeness of his resurrection" (Rom. 6:5).

The life everlasting: "Now if we be dead with Christ, we believe that we shall also live with him" (Rom. 6:8).

Renewal and cleansing: "According to his mercy, he saved us by the washing of regeneration, and renewing of the Holy Ghost" (Titus 3:5).

The unity of the faith: "For by one Spirit we are all baptized into one body" (1 Cor. 12:13).

NOTE 1.—The beauty, impressiveness, and general effect of the sacred rite of baptism are not a little affected by the manner of its administration. It should be so carefully arranged, and performed with such propriety that no mistakes could occur. If the administrator is calm, self-possessed, acting under a sense of the importance and solemnity of the occasion, the candidate will usually be calm and free from agitation. The spiritual effect on the candidate and observers depends on the dignity and propriety of administration.

NOTE 2.—Baptism is usually administered by ordained ministers. And this is proper, regular, and orderly. But should occasion require, and the church so direct, it would be equally valid if administered by a deacon or any private member selected for that service. The validity depends on the character and profession of the candidate, and not on that of the administrator. The New Testament is silent as to the qualifications of administrators, except that they were disciples.

NOTE 3.—Baptism, strictly speaking, is not to be repeated. But cases may be discovered in which it had been administered to candidates who had not at that time experienced a saving faith in Christ, and had not made an intelligent confession of such faith. In such cases baptism may be repeated when the candidate becomes duly qualified. This would be rebaptizing in form, but not in fact, since, in the former case, a lack of faith made the act invalid. Such cases seldom occur, and, when they do, can be mutually adjusted by the candidate and the church.

B. THE LORD'S SUPPER

The Lord's Supper (also called the Communion or the Eucharist) is the other ordinance established by Christ, and ordained to be observed in his churches till the end of time. It has equal simplicity and impressiveness with baptism, but represents a different phase of vital doctrine. This, perhaps even more than baptism, has been the occasion of heated and often bitter controversy among the professed followers of Christ, through the ages of history.

1. *Its Institution*

The Supper is thus described in the Bible: "For I have received of the Lord that which also I delivered unto you, that the Lord Jesus the same night in which he was betrayed took bread: And when he had given thanks, he brake it, and said, Take, eat: this is my body, which is broken for you: This do in remembrance of me. After the same manner also he took the cup, when he had supped, saying, This cup is the new testament in my blood: This do ye, as oft as ye drink it, in remembrance of me. For as often as ye eat this bread, and drink this cup, ye do show the Lord's death till he come" (1 Cor. 11:23-26; see also Matt. 26:26-30, Mark 14:22-26, Luke 22:14-20).

It was at the close of (or immediately following) the passover supper, which was the seal of the old covenant, now passed away and sanctified by the sacrifice of the paschal lamb, that Jesus inaugurated his own memorial as a seal of the new covenant and a memorial of the sacrifice of the Lamb of God, who taketh away the sins of the world. The sad, tender, and sacred associations of the time and the place have all passed into history, and are reproduced in the hearts of all true and loving disciples, as they surround the table of their Lord.

2. *Its Administration*

The Supper is a provision of bread and wine—the *loaf* and the *cup*—as symbols of Christ's body and blood, partaken of by the members of the church assembled, to commemorate his sufferings and death for them, and to show their faith and participation in his sacrifice.

The pastor serves the bread and the cup, preceding each with a brief prayer of thanksgiving, as did the Lord. He passes the plates and cups in order to the deacons, who distribute to the members. It is customary to partake only after all have been served.

It is a common practice to receive a fellowship offering at this service, which is administered by the deacons for the care of the sick and needy and for other special causes.

The service is usually closed with a fellowship hymn, such as "Blest Be the Tie that Binds," after the manner of Jesus and the Apostles: "And when they had sung an hymn, they went out into the Mount of Olives" (Matt. 26:30).

3. Its Obligation

It is a sacred privilege for every Christian to remember his Lord in the observance of the Supper, and it is his solemn duty as well. "Take, eat . . . drink ye all of it" (Matt. 26:26-27) . "This do in remembrance of me" (Luke 22:19). Such were the words of Jesus himself. Let no disciple who loves his Lord esteem lightly or neglect this sacred rite.

4. Its Subjects

Historically, there are two views as to who may partake of the Lord's Supper. These are known as *open* and *close communion*. Open communion is that which permits any one who desires, and believes himself qualified, to come to the Lord's table, without any questions being asked, or conditions imposed by the church where the communion is observed. Close communion, on the other hand, is restricted to immersed believers who are members in good standing of Baptist churches. Although the latter practice is strictly maintained in many churches in the South, practically all northern churches and some southern churches now practice open communion.[2]

5. *Its Significance*

It was designed to commemorate the death of Christ for human redemption, and to be a perpetual memorial in his churches and to his people of his sacrifice for men. The *loaf* and the *cup* represent his broken body and his shed blood, as sealing the covenant of grace.

The Supper also points the Christian onward to the triumph and glory of Christ's second coming. Thus it is a kind of mediator, a middle link, binding the shadowy past, the radiant future, and the joyous present in one. He who was dead is alive again; the sufferings of death could not hold him. The past lays the foundation of the Christian's hope, while the future holds the bright fruition. "But I say unto you, I will not drink henceforth of this fruit of the vine, until that day when I drink it new with you in my Father's kingdom" (Matt. 26:29). "For as often as ye eat this bread, and drink this cup, ye do show the Lord's death till he come" (1 Cor. 11:26).

The Supper is also a teacher of vital gospel doctrine, such as:

The love of Christ as a seal of the testament of grace, and of his faithfulness to them that trust him:

[2] In this respect, there has been a change in practice since the days of Dr. Hiscox, who unequivocally called close communion "the Baptist view," and argued strenuously against open communion (*The New Directory for Baptist Churches,* pp. 450-453).

"This cup is the new testament in my blood" (Luke 22:20).

The union of all Christian believers with their Lord: "The cup of blessing which we bless, is it not the communion of the blood of Christ? The bread which we break, is it not the communion of the body of Christ?" (1 Cor. 10:16).

The unity of Christians under the leadership of Christ: "For we, being many, are one bread, and one body, for we are all partakers of that one bread" (1 Cor. 10:17).

Spiritual life and nourishment as derived from Christ: "For ye are dead, and your life is hid with Christ in God" (Col. 3:3). "For even Christ, our passover, is sacrificed for us. Therefore let us keep the feast; not with old leaven . . . but with the unleavened bread of sincerity and truth" (1 Cor. 5:7, 8).

Christ as the only and abounding fountain of grace. "I am the living bread which came down from heaven; if any man eat of this bread, he shall live forever: and the bread that I will give is my flesh, which I will give for the life of the world" (John 6:51).

NOTE 1.—As in the case of baptism, the Supper is commonly and properly administered by the pastor, or some other ordained and accredited minister. But should occasion require, and the church so direct, it would be just as valid if served by a deacon, or any other devout member.

NOTE 2.—The deacons usually and properly distribute the elements. But any member can be called on for that service, should occasion require, and the service would be as valid.

Note 3.—When Jesus said, "This is my body," and "This is my blood," he did not mean, and could not have intended, it in a literal sense, since his body and his blood at that moment were not in the loaf and cup, but in his corporeal person. He must, therefore, have meant what Protestant Christendom holds, generally, that he did mean, namely, that these elements *represented* his body and blood. There is, therefore, no transubstantiation, or change of elements, and the bread and wine, when received by the communicant, are literally the same as before their use and distribution, and nothing different.

Note 4.—The hand of fellowship is usually given to new members at this service, just before the distribution of the elements. This act is simply a fraternal welcome, and has no other significance; it does not make them members, but only recognizes their membership, already effected by church vote.

Note 5.—Many pastors, before the ordinance, give an invitation for "members of sister churches" or "members of churches of the same faith and order" who might be present, to remain and partake with them. But some pastors give no invitation at all. It is not, however, the right of the pastor to give or to withhold any invitation, except as the church directs. It is the prerogative of the body to decide that question. The pastor should assume no responsibility in the matter, but let it all rest with the church. He is their servant, not their master, in these matters.

Note 6.—Since the Supper is distinctively a church ordinance, it is to be observed by churches only and not by individuals (even though church members), neither in private places, nor in sickrooms, nor on social occasions, and not by companies of disciples other than churches, though composed of church members. But a church may by appointment, meet in a private house, a sickroom, or wherever it may elect, and there observe the ordinance. Therefore, in such instances, the pastor is accompanied at least by one or more deacons representing the congregation as a whole.

NOTE 7.—There is no scriptural rule as to the frequency with which, nor the time or place at which, it shall be observed. The primitive Christians evidently kept this feast daily. Subsequently it came to be a weekly service, at each public assembly. By some it is still so observed. Some churches observe it quarterly, some bimonthly; but with our people it has come to be a general custom to have the Communion monthly, and usually on the first Sunday in the month. This is not so often as to impair its sanctity by frequency, and not so seldom as to allow it to pass out of mind and be forgotten.

NOTE 8.—Pastors should instruct their members as to the nature, significance, and claims of the Lord's Supper. The people should be well taught as to the meaning of the ordinance, and its true relation to their faith and spiritual life.

CHAPTER VI

CHRISTIAN WORSHIP

WORSHIP, properly speaking, is adoration and
praise offered to God. The emotion, instinctive in a
dedicated Christian, tends to exalt and magnify him
to whom all honor and glory are due. It is offered in
response to the glorious excellence of the divine
character, and also because of what God has done for
men—both for what he is, and for what he does. It
usually includes confession for sin and supplication
for pardon.

Worship is an important duty and a gracious
privilege. But no act of devotion can be acceptable
to him, unless it be spontaneous and sincere. If it be
so, he delights in it and accepts it with pleasure from
his creatures. Its influence on the spiritual life of the
individual and that of the church, as well as the
moral sense of the community, can be great.

A. PREACHING

Preaching, strictly speaking, is not worship,

though calculated to inspire and assist worship. Preaching is a proclamation of truth, not an address to the Deity. The preacher is a herald (*kerux*), a proclaimer, and his address (*kerugma*), a message delivered to an audience.

The true object and design of preaching is to bring people to Christ and to help them grow in their Christian discipleship. Instruction may properly be said to be the first object of preaching. Most emphatically it is not to entertain an audience, nor to crowd the house with hearers, nor to build up wealthy and fashionable congregations, nor to replenish the treasury, nor to teach literature, science, or art, but to save and nurture souls by an exhibition of Christ crucified. For this purpose our Lord designated "some, pastors and teachers, for the perfecting of the saints, for the work of the ministry, for the edifying of the body of Christ" (Eph. 4:11, 12).

Preaching should be plain and simple in style, spiritual in tone, experimental and practical in substance. The very basis and foundation of every sermon should be *instruction*. In the outline of the sermon, the parts should follow each other by a natural sequence, so that the hearers will easily understand their relationship. As to the style, clarity is of the first importance. The speaker is not preaching in an unknown tongue, and every sentence and word should be so clear in its meaning that none can misunderstand. Nevertheless, the more interesting and attractive the preaching, the more welcome and useful it is likely to prove.

B. PRAYER

Prayer is an important element in Christian life, both individual and social. "Ask, and it shall be given you; seek, and ye shall find; knock, and it shall be opened unto you," was the positive declaration of our Lord to his disciples (Matt. 7:7). As to group prayer, "If two of you shall agree on earth, as touching anything that they shall ask, it shall be done for them of my Father which is in heaven" (Matt. 18:19). Likewise, private prayer is essential to the soul's spiritual life, and is encouraged by the promise of special blessing: "But thou, when thou prayest, enter into thy closet, and when thou hast shut thy door, pray to thy Father which is in secret; and thy Father which seeth in secret shall reward thee openly" (Matt. 6:6).

1. *Leading in Prayer*

Prayer adjusts itself in form to varying occasions. The pastor's prayer before his congregation would speak for them as well as for himself and would be different from his prayer in his own study, at the family altar, in the sickroom, with a penitent sinner, or with a dying saint. The prayer before the sermon would naturally differ from that at its close.

Yet in spirit all prayer is essentially the same. He who prays is supposed to shut out the world, and become unaware of anything else while he communes with God. It includes adoration, confession, thanksgiving, and supplication, and recognizes the intercession of Christ. "Whatsoever ye shall ask the

Father in my name, he will give it you" (John 16:23).

There needs to be adequate preparation, in order to lead others in prayer to the mercy seat—not a preparation of words, but of the heart; not a forethought of phrases for that particular occasion, but a spirit in harmony with the divine fullness and a *felt* necessity for the blessings sought. He who would have this preparation when in the pulpit must obtain it before he goes there. "He that cometh to God must believe that he is, and that he is a rewarder of them that diligently seek him" (Heb. 11:6). "But let him ask in faith, nothing wavering" (James 1:6).

To *make* prayers and to *pray*, are very different things. Anyone who can command the use of language can make a prayer; but to pray the soul must commune with God. There is constant danger that prayers offered in the pulpit will become stereotyped and monotonous, so constantly are they repeated, and under circumstances so almost exactly similar. The best preventive is a fervent spirit, and a deep sense of the need of divine assistance.

Prayer should be simple, direct, and brief. It should be so simple in style that all in the assembly can intelligently unite in it. It should be direct as to what is prayed for, and not wander over all possible subjects, seeking nothing in particular, and expecting nothing in particular. It should be *brief*: of course, in some cases more so than in others. The "long prayer" is a calamity to both the minister and the people. It is often difficult to perform and painful to endure, and often it is not prayer at all, but a religious address.

Prayers should be distinctly uttered, so that all can understand and unite in them; nor should there be anything, in manner or expression, so peculiar as to divert the thoughts of hearers from the devotion. Especially should the petitioner "use not vain repetitions, as the heathen do; for they think that they shall be heard for their much speaking" (Matt. 6:7). The whole style and manner should be penitential, reverent, and dignified, savoring of meekness and humility, as is becoming in sinful, helpless creatures when approaching a holy God.

It may seem a most ungracious thing to criticize so sacred an exercise as prayer ought to be, and to point out defects which not unfrequently mar its excellencies. The one prevailing defect, no doubt, is the want of faith, of spirituality, and of the influence of the Holy Spirit. There are, however, certain defects into which the pious sometimes unconsciously fall, which deserve attention and correction. Here are some common faults:

Preaching Prayers, in which Scripture is explained, doctrine expounded, and instruction offered to the audience.

Exhorting Prayers, where warnings, rebukes, and exhortations seem addressed to classes or individuals, and possibly personal sins are pointed out.

Historical Prayers, in which facts and incidents are related, from which inferences and arguments are adduced. (Not to be commended, though David, Solomon, and Ezra indulged in them on very special occasions!)

Oratorical Prayers, which seem framed with special

regard to the language, as if intended for critical ears.

Complimentary Prayers, where the excellencies of persons present or absent are effectively dwelt on, as if individuals were flattered, rather than the Deity worshiped.

Fault-finding Prayers, which make prominent the real or fancied faults of the church or of individuals, existing difficulties deplored, advice given, remedies suggested, or rebukes administered.

All such things should be avoided.

2. *The Prayer Meeting*

As the services of evangelical churches generally are arranged, the prayer meeting comes in the middle of the week. As a rule it is not numerously attended. But the most spiritual and devout members attend; and those who do habitually attend become the devout and spiritually minded, if they were not such before. This service not only reveals, but nourishes and develops the religious vitality of the church, and its importance as a spiritual force cannot well be overestimated. The pastor who is wise for the good of his people will cultivate this part of worship.

Doubtless every pastor believes himself fully capable of so ordering this service as to produce the best results, without advice from any one. And yet it is probably safe to say that not one minister in ten knows how to make a prayer meeting effective, and about one in twenty would kill the best one that could be put into his hands. The following suggestions—a few out of many—may be helpful to some:

1. The success and utility of the prayer meeting

depends on the leader, more than on any other one thing, save the presence of the Holy Spirit. The leader will presumably be the pastor. He certainly ought not to commit the management of so important a matter to other hands, as a rule. And he ought to give diligence and prayerful study to bring this department of worship to the highest possible state of interest and efficiency.

2. The success of the service does not depend on the numbers who attend. Though a full meeting is desirable, yet a very full meeting may be a very poor one, and a very small meeting may be a very good one.

3. The prayer meeting is not a "teaching service." Though its exercises will convey instruction, yet instruction is not its special function. That belongs to the pulpit, the Bible class, and other similar exercises. This is for the heart rather than for the intellect. It is to feed the spiritual hunger of the soul, to cheer, inspire, comfort.

4. Singing should have a large place in the prayer meeting. The hymns should be wisely adjusted to the service and the temper of the occasion and so familiar that all can use them.

5. Begin the meeting on time. That will help the attendants to be prompt. If the leader waits for the people, the people will be all the later. Train them to habits of punctuality. And do not continue so long as to exhaust the interest, and have to stop on a falling tide.

6. Have the place of meeting pleasant, comfortable, and attractive. Worshipers, especially the

young, should associate beauty, purity, and good order with religion. Be sure to have plenty of pure air and good light in the prayer room.

7. As the chief value and potency of the meeting lies in its spiritual atmosphere, one of the chief subjects of prayer should be the implored presence and aid of the Holy Spirit.

C. Sacred Music

The power and influence of sacred song in worship are not understood and appreciated as they ought to be. Even where music is highly cultivated in Christian congregations, the interest is too often artistic rather than spiritual. Music may become high art in the house of God, but that does not make it worship. Of course it should be artistic in the best sense of that term, but only that it may be the more devout. In the old temple service of the Hebrews, music, together with sacrifices and offerings, constituted almost their only worship.

Indeed in our less pretentious Christian services, singing constitutes almost the only act that can be called worship in the strictest sense. Like prayer, the service of song may express adoration, confession, supplication and praise. But, unlike prayer, all can vocally unite in this act of worship. Now, as in the primitive churches, the people can worship "in psalms and hymns and spiritual songs, singing and making melody in [their] heart to the Lord" (Eph. 5:19).

Worship through music is a pleasant privilege,

which animates the dull and soothes the agitated spirit. While it comforts and inspires the saints, it, more than any other part of religious service, attracts the unconverted and the unbelieving. It is the act of worship in which all occupy a common attitude, and mutually bear a part. It is not, therefore, strange that sacred song has occupied so large a place in the history of Christian worship, and that the affections of the renewed heart cherish it so fondly, and resort to it so constantly. Christianity has sung its triumphs through the ages, and around the world.

Church music should be primarily the united expression of the assembly—the worship of all uttered in song. It is not a performance by a company of musicians for the entertainment of the congregation, but an act of worship by the congregation itself. It is not to be an act of worship performed by others, to which the people are to listen, but an act of worship which they themselves are to offer. "Let the people praise thee, O God: let all the people praise thee" (Ps. 67:5).

Since the true idea of sacred song is that the people shall worship, not witness a performance, the style of music should be such as the people can perform.

A great variety in style and execution may be very well introduced in one or two anthems, chants, or sentences by the choir. But the hymns should be sung to simple music, so familiar that the people can sing them without an effort to remember the tune, and without danger of losing it, all thought being given to the sentiment and spirit of the words.

CHAPTER VII

THE CHURCH'S WITNESS

CHURCHES are God's appointed agencies for the salvation of men. Though it would be false to say that men could not be saved outside the churches, and without their aid, yet, as a matter of fact, such is rarely the case.

The mission of a Christian church, therefore, is to a "world lying in wickedness," to men "dead in trespasses and sins," as the bearer of glad tidings to "prisoners of hope," and herald of the great salvation to lost men. In order to accomplish this, the church must maintain the faith and discipline, the order and ordinances of the gospel. Indeed, for this cause Christ gave himself for the church, "that he might present it to himself a glorious church, not having spot or wrinkle, or any such thing; but that it should be holy and without blemish" (Eph. 5:27). A self-centered and materialistic church can never perform this holy mission; indeed, it is neither worthy of it, nor fitted for it.

The responsibility of a church is both corporate and personal. As a *body* it is to make its influence felt far and near. Each member, therefore, should strive to be and to do what the entire church ought to be and do, "the light of the world," "the salt of the earth," "a city set on a hill, that cannot be hid." There is work for all, and work adapted to the condition and ability and capacity of each, old and young, great and small, male and female. The efficiency and usefulness of a church depend on each member's doing his own work, so as neither to attempt the work of others, nor yet to stand idly by while others serve. In nothing, perhaps, are the wisdom and skill of the pastor and officers more apparent than in finding suitable work for all.

It is a sad and somewhat humiliating reflection that so many churches exert so small an influence on their communities. The moral influence of these institutions of Christianity ought to do more to repress evil, and to increase righteousness. The results of church life and action are often more apparent in the lands of the younger churches overseas than in our own country. Doubtless the explanation of this is to be found in the lack of vitality of Christian faith and life among us.

Some common methods of Christian work are as follows:

A. PROCLAMATION OF THE GOSPEL

The preaching of the gospel, the proclamation of pardon and eternal life through faith in Christ, is the

foremost and the most effective instrumentality for
the salvation of the world. It is divinely ordained,
and divinely sanctioned and sustained. The command is, "Go ye into all the world, and preach the
gospel to every creature" (Mark 16:15). The promise
is, "My word . . . shall not return unto me void, but
it shall accomplish that which I please, and it shall
prosper in the thing whereto I sent it" (Isaiah 55:11).
Four types of situations which provide opportunities
for preaching may be noted:

1. Every church will support its own evangelical
preaching ministry for the instruction and conversion
of all who may be attracted to it. This ministry
should be able and faithful, and generously sustained.
If the nations are to be fed, the family at home must
be built up and instructed in the purposes of grace.

2. At certain times, special preaching missions or
evangelistic campaigns seem demanded, special occasions indicated by the Spirit's movement, and an
unusual disposition on the part of the people to give
heed to spiritual and eternal concerns.

3. Within the range of many churches, there are
certain institutions, such as prisons, mental hospitals,
or nursing homes, whose residents cannot or do not
attend the churches. If they are to have the gospel it
must be carried to them. And often they are more
ready and eager hearers of the word than stated congregations.

4. But the world is the field, whose bounds extend
beyond home and country and kindred. Begin at
Jerusalem, but do not stop till *all nations* are reached,
and every creature taught the way of life through

Christ crucified. Each church and each individual should feel his obligation to aid in sending the gospel to people *the world over*. That was Christ's purpose and design. For that he died. Those who have his spirit will strive to carry forward the work he began; "if any man have not the spirit of Christ, he is none of his" (Rom. 8:9).

NOTE 1.—Great good has been effected by a few churches, in developing and putting to use lay preaching. In almost every church are brethren who possess more than ordinary gifts for interpreting the Scriptures, addressing congregations, and conducting religious meetings.

B. RELIGIOUS VISITATION

Religious visitation is an effective means by which the churches can further their mission among the families of the neighborhoods they serve, especially those families which have no church relationships, and who therefore are under no definite religious influence.

It is presumed, of course, that the minister will visit such households, and offer them religious guidance and counseling. But this is not enough. The church, under the leadership of the pastor, should adopt some plan for systematic religious visitation carried on by the lay members. Such a plan may serve a variety of purposes, for example (1) to invite them to the house of God, and bring the children into the Sunday school; (2) if in sickness, want, or other misfortune, to report the fact to the church, and furnish such relief as may be practicable; (3) to provide a ministry of friendship to the sick and to those who mourn; and (4) to invite individuals to accept Christ and unite with his church (lay visitation evangelism). Thus the reality of the Christian fellowship can be demonstrated to those who do not know it.

In no other way can Christians more effectually imitate their Lord and Master, who "went about doing good," relieving and removing the temporal sufferings of men, that he might effectually reach their souls with spiritual food. There is no more Christly mission for the churches than this, and every member can bear some part in it. Hearts oppressed with sorrow hunger for sympathy, and welcome the counsels of those who will give it.

This ministry of Christian faith and love cannot well be overestimated in its value, both to those who perform it, and to those who receive it. James was right: "Pure religion and undefiled before God and the Father is this, to visit the fatherless and widows in their affliction, and to keep himself unspotted from the world" (James 1:27). And yet how few of God's people appreciate this work, or are anxious to imitate this most notable feature of the life and character of Jesus!

As to the *method* for this service:

1. Let the whole area which the church considers its responsibility be divided into districts, and a certain number of families be apportioned to each man or woman who is willing to undertake the service; or, let them go "two and two," which is better, and according to the apostolic plan. Let these visitors

report the results of their mission, from time to time, in the midweek meetings of the church, or at specially designated times, and at the end of the year make a full report of the work done, and the realized results. Such reports will not only be interesting, but cannot fail to stimulate Christian activity through the entire body.

2. If the church as a whole cannot be moved to such a service, then let the few who are willing agree among themselves to attempt it. Perhaps it may be a project of the deacons and deaconesses. The Lord will bless the endeavor, and their success will stimulate others. Should there be but one or two who are willing, let them try the blessed service, and spread the result before the church. The Lord can work by few, as well as by many. "And he that reapeth receiveth wages, and gathereth fruit unto life eternal" (John 4:36).

C. CHRISTIAN LITERATURE

Another practicable and effective means for bringing religious truth in contact with human minds is the use of the printed page. Every good book or periodical put into circulation is a personal and a public blessing, and this means of grace is so accessible that none need be without it. Aside from the periodical religious press, there are numerous societies whose only business is the publication and circulation of religious reading at prices within the reach of all. Our own, as well as other Christian denominations, has its publication society, doing nobly and

well this work, and deserving the utmost confidence
and the largest patronage.

1. *A few good religious books* should be in every
home. A few, read over and over until the mind is
thoroughly imbued with their spirit, are better than
many carelessly read, or not read at all. Many Christian families, it is a pity to say, have a generous supply
of secular books in their homes, but few or none at
all of a religious nature.

2. *Church libraries* are an excellent means for in-
tellectual and religious instruction (see page 123).

3. *Religious periodicals* are, if possible, still more
important than books, not in their intrinsic worth
indeed, but because they are so much more easily
obtained, and so much more likely to be read. Few
things could become so great a help to a pastor in his
pulpit and pastoral work as a really good religious
paper in every family. A reliable denominational
paper should be in the home of every church family.
It is certainly a shame for Baptists not to know what
is going on among their own people.

D. Missionary Support

Christianity is the most emphatic missionary force
in the world, and every Christian church is a divinely
appointed missionary society. If every church could
be fully true to the purpose for which it was instituted, no other missionary organizations would be
needed to send the gospel of the blessed God to the
ends of the earth. In apostolic history, no others were
known, and yet they went everywhere preaching

Christ, and filled the world with the gospel of his salvation. Every church and every disciple is under bonds to Christ to aid in carrying out the great commission, "Go ye into all the world, and preach the gospel to every creature" (Mark 16:15). No church can hope for prosperity at home unless it strives to give the means of salvation to all men.

Because it is not practicable in our day for all to go out into the world as career missionaries, Christians may avail themselves of the alternative of contributing financially to the support of those who do go. There are, of course, many who say that they have hard work to sustain their own church, and therefore cannot help others. This, however, is false reasoning. They that withhold from others who need, dry up the fountains of their benevolence, and have less for themselves, instead of more. God, who alone can give the increase, prospers those who trust and honor him. The churches that do not sympathize with, and aid missionary endeavor, are not likely to be very flourishing or prosperous. The missionary churches are uniformly the most honored and useful, whether rich or poor, large or small.

We have our missionary societies on a national scale for both home and foreign Christian service, doing grand and most effective work, and having a long and honorable history of good deeds and noble successes. They possess resources for the most effective and economical prosecution of their gracious enterprises. Their service commands our confidence, and we know their work is in harmony with gospel purposes. The churches should give these societies their sympathies, their prayers, and their generous financial support. Thereby they help to give the knowledge of salvation to those beyond the reach of their individual endeavors. The success which has attended the missionary work of American Baptists, through these societies, both in our own country, and in foreign lands, is most amazing, and testifies unmistakably to God's blessing on the work, and the favor with which he regards the methods that have been pursued.

In all that is said or may be said, it must be constantly borne in mind that a very large responsibility does and necessarily must rest on the pastors. For such purposes is the pastor made overseer of the flock, to instruct in duty as well as in privilege, and lead on to the discharge of every obligation. Few churches will be missionary churches if the pastors feel no interest in such work, and do not stimulate them, propose plans, impart information, and lead the people forward. With a pastor to do this faithfully, few churches would fail or fall short of a good degree of effectiveness.

E. Social Concern

To what extent should a church relate itself to the various movements for civic and social betterment which are found in practically every area? These vary in their purpose and scope from one community to another, and also from one generation to another. They include such groups as temperance societies, organizations for world peace, movements against gambling, and bodies concerned with the welfare of children, youth, the aged, or minority groups.

A church is a society emphatically concerned with carrying out God's will for a better community, both locally and throughout the world. And no person should be admitted to, or retained in, its fellowship who will not both agree to, and walk by, this rule. If the churches were loyal to their duty and true to their mission, they could do more for the suppression of immorality and the encouragement of the general welfare than any other organization. But some causes can be better served by distinct organizations, where all are of one mind concerning the object to be accomplished. For example, it must be confessed, however embarrassingly, that in some churches there are members, who, for personal reasons, do not like to hear much said on the temperance question, and some ministers who lack courage to say much on it. Often, therefore, a temperance society will speak with a clearer voice than a church.

Since churches, as such, cannot identify themselves organically with other societies, they should in every consistent way give their moral support to encourage such endeavors, as well as pray for their success. All that any such society professes, the church professes; and the church professes more—not only to conserve the morals of society, but to save the souls of men. Only let the churches be true to their profession. They can well give their "Godspeed" to every individual, and to every organization which honestly strives to do good in the world.

F. CHRISTIAN EDUCATION[1]

Churches should provide religious instruction for the children and youth of their own families, and for the children and youth of other families who may be disposed to avail themselves of the privilege. Adult education also should not be overlooked. This instruction should prominently include Bible study and the application of biblical principles to contemporary life.

An adequate program of Christian education will include a wide range of opportunities for study including many or all of the following, and under the general direction of an elected board of Christian education:

Sunday church school
Sunday evening fellowship
Vacation church school
Weekday religious education
Leadership education classes
School of missions
Summer camps and conferences
Discipleship classes
Church library
Special activities

Each of these will be discussed briefly in this chapter; for more detailed suggestions and information, the church is advised to consult publications of the Baptist convention of which the church is a member.

---

[1] This is a new section, not included in any of Dr. Hiscox's works, but added here in view of the tremendous growth of interest in this subject since his time.

1. Sunday Church School

At one time, the Sunday church school was almost the only means of Christian education; it is still probably the one which reaches the largest number of people. It has a threefold influence: Directly upon the pupils themselves, indirectly upon the homes from which they come, and reflectively upon the officers and teachers who work with them. Thus, a consecrated, well-administered, and well-taught school has great potential for carrying out the church's mission.

It is increasingly the practice to regard this institution as a teaching arm of the church, an integral part of the program, administration, and budget of the church. Hence its curriculum and activities are planned to carry out the purposes of the church, its superintendent is an elected officer of the church, and its funds are handled by the church treasurer. Thus the budget for the school is not necessarily balanced in itself; in some churches, the school will be able to contribute more to the church through its offerings than it receives, whereas in others its requirements will be greater than it is able to give.

Church school curriculum materials should be adopted by the church's board of Christian education, and the same curriculum should be throughout the school. No catch-as-catch-can, everybody-choose-his-own assortment of teaching materials can possibly provide a balanced curriculum with adequate emphasis on each of the major parts of the Bible and each significant area of human need. In choosing curriculum materials, the board has two sets of options—(1) whether to use "graded" or "uniform" lessons and (2) whether to adopt those of his own denomination, some other denomination, or an independent publisher.

As to the first option, uniform lessons are produced according to an interdenominational plan for studying a cross-section of the entire Bible simultaneously at all age levels in a six-year cycle. By this plan, all members of the family are studying the same Bible passage on a given day, with application at the level of their own needs (except when the subject matter is unsuitable for children, in which case there are minor variations). Graded lessons, on the other hand, make no pretense of uniformity, but contain subject matter selected according to the interests and needs of the age-group. Both types of lessons therefore blend Bible study with life applications, but with a somewhat different focus.

The second option, denominational vs. independent publishers, must also be faced by the board of Christian education. In making this decision, it will do well to recognize that the missionary work of its own Baptist convention will be highlighted in denominational materials and largely ignored in those of independent publishers or other denominations; also, that distinctive denominational doctrines such as believers' baptism must of necessity be slighted in the independent materials because of the wide range of users to whom they are sold. It is also a factor that the denominational publisher is a non-profit and missionary institution in a special way, in that proceeds from the production and sale of curriculum materials by denominational publishers are used to help pay for state and national field programs of Christian education serving the churches they represent.

The Sunday church school session varies in length in different churches, but there is much to be said for the expanded session, in which the younger children have all or part (depending on their age group) of the church worship hour for a continuation of their learning experiences. In some churches this period is referred to as "junior church." The better church school curriculum materials include resources for the expanded session.

2. *Sunday Evening Fellowship*

The Sunday evening youth fellowship has been a familiar activity in our churches for many years, sometimes as a single group, again as separate age groups for junior high, senior high, and older youth. More recently, the plan of an all-church fellowship on Sunday evening has developed, with groups also for adults and for children of various ages. The evening hour, with its atmosphere of informality, allows for a more creative type of program than that of Sunday morning. In some churches, the traditional Sunday evening preaching service is held after the fellowship groups; in others, it is condensed into a brief service of worship in which all ages may participate. Helps for program and administration of a Sunday evening fellowship may be obtained from denominational Christian education staffs.

3. *Vacation Church School*

The vacation church school provides an opportunity for Christian education in a more concentrated period of time than any other except camping and conferences. Generally running for two five-day weeks, two to three hours a day, it thus allows from twenty to thirty hours of time, so that intensive instruction with a good share of creative activity may be offered. Dramatics, art projects, and handicrafts are further encouraged by the fact that the pupils are usually dressed in informal summer play clothes which they would not consider suitable on Sunday morning. Vacation church schools provide excellent evangelistic opportunities, as they often attract children who have not participated in the Sunday program at all. Often, churches of different denominations will cooperate in a neighborhood school, each providing pupils and teachers; the classes meet in the largest, most central, or best-equipped church building, or (better still) different grades meet in different buildings.

4. *Weekday Religious Education*

Known also as "released time," weekday religious education is a program of Christian instruction of public school pupils during an hour a week in which they are excused from other classes for the purpose of receiving this special work in the church of their choice. Thus, Protestant, Catholic, and Jewish children may all receive weekday religious education simultaneously at their appropriate buildings and from persons of their own faith. Some Baptist churches give released-time instruction independently, but many do so in conjunction with other evangelical churches, perhaps under sponsorship of the local council of churches. It is particularly important that well qualified persons be selected for this type of teaching, since comparison with public school teachers is inevitable in the minds of the pupils. Recommendations as to curriculum materials for released time may be secured from denominational Christian education staff personnel.

5. *Leadership Education Classes*

It is important that church leadership, especially in Christian education, be well trained for their work. When such is the case, they do their jobs better and enjoy them more. They need to be well versed both in general backgrounds, such as the Bible, theology, social problems, etc. ("enrichment courses") and specific techniques for handling their own responsibilities in the church ("methods courses"). Leadership education courses can be taught within the local church, but often associational or community leadership schools are preferred. There is a standard curriculum of approved courses and texts and a procedure for certifying qualified teachers of such courses, which can be ascertained from your denominational department of leadership education.

6. *School of Missions*

The most intensive form of missionary education in the local church is probably the school of missions. This is an organized opportunity for the whole church to focus its interest and attention on one area of study. It is in reality a total congregational gathering on a certain night each week over a predetermined number of weeks to study a specific home or overseas mission theme. In a minimum effort there are at least three groupings—children, youth, and adults—in classes, although a more complete grading is preferable for study. The family as a whole can unite for part of the evening in worship, fellowship, and special features.

7. *Summer Camps and Conferences*

Special summertime programs at a denominational or interdenominational camp or conference center provide an experience of Christian living which can be as important as the material studied, or more so. As an encouragement, many churches find it wise to pay part of the expenses of those who attend, not just as "representatives," but to provide them with a type of Christian education not available in the local church itself. Some churches have been experimenting with their own day camping programs which have most of the characteristics of resident camping but fewer problems.

8. *Discipleship Classes*

The training of persons who have accepted Christ but have not yet become church members—as well as those who are inquirers and, after training, may accept him—is also a function of Christian education. Preferably conducted by the pastor if possible, but otherwise by carefully selected lay persons, such classes meet weekly for several weeks before baptism and reception into membership, providing a study of basic Christian doctrine and denominational and local church practices. Such classes should not include too wide an age span. Separate groups for juniors, junior highs, senior highs, and adults are recommended, even when the "group" is only one person receiving private instruction from the pastor.

9. *Church Library*

Recognition of the church library as an instrument of Christian education is relatively recent. The old-time church library, with its collection of Tom Swift, the Five Little Peppers, and a few assorted Joseph C. Lincoln books, mingled with such items as *Beautiful Joe* and *In His Steps*, valuable as it may have been in its day, is not the educational library which alert churches are now developing. Today's church library should include a variety of reference works on the Bible and Christian thought, books on aspects of church work and witness which members may be called on to do, and some serious and reasonably current religious fiction and non-fiction to challenge thinking and stimulate spiritual growth. It is not primarily a children's library, but mainly for adults and seriously inclined young people. The children will find reading books in their own church school departments.

10. *Special Activities*

This last category is included, not so much to suggest other specific forms which Christian education may take, as to serve as a reminder that there are still other possibilities unmentioned, and that the church which is sensitive to its responsibilities will constantly search for new ways in which to make the word of God meaningful to people in daily living.

G. The Wider Fellowship of Baptists[2]

Because churches are the only Christian organizations provided for in the New Testament, it may be said that they are the only ones really essential to the accomplishment of the purposes of Christ. Experience, however, has demonstrated that churches in fellowship with one another are able to fulfill the work of the gospel more effectively than churches alone. This section will deal with some of the ways in which Baptists share this fellowship with one another. No effort will be made to discuss in any detail the various organizations in which they may cooperate with churches of other denominations.

1. *Associations*

It is customary for churches in a limited area, small enough that their members can easily come together for meetings, to work together through Baptist associations. These churches agree to cooperate in the association, and meet yearly, with one of their number as host. These meetings are usually attended by the pastors and a certain number of laymen as representatives or messengers. Others, of course, are also welcome to attend as visitors. At this meeting, some of the time is occupied in hearing reports from the various churches—each one sending with the messengers a letter, setting forth their condition as to anything of special interest to themselves or to the body. Sermons are preached, mis-

[2] The material in this section has been substantially revised from the original Hiscox texts, because of vast changes which have taken place since they were written.

sionary addresses delivered, and special topics considered in Christian education, evangelism, social concern, and other areas of mutual interest. New pastors and new churches are welcomed. Rallies or conferences of men, women, and youth as separate groups may be included. There may be a presentation by one or more persons from the state convention. Various business matters are also considered.

These annual gatherings constitute not only favorable opportunities for projecting plans for missionary work within the bounds of the association, but they also give occasion for members of the various churches to make and renew friendships which strengthen the fellowship of Baptists in the area.

In addition to its annual meeting, the association also serves churches at other times of the year. Men's, women's, and young people's organizations, as well as ministerial groups related to the association, hold various meetings for inspiration, study, and fellowship. Some associations have a mid-year rally, when some speaker of wide appeal comes to the area to address a large congregation composed of many worshipers from the various churches of the association. Associational committees may continue to carry out the work of this fellowship between annual meetings (as through Christian education conferences and cooperative visitation evangelism efforts). Most associations have some continuing relationship to ordination standards and procedures, perhaps through a permanent council or committee on ordination.

The largest associations, particularly those serving major metropolitan areas, often have professionally trained staff workers, such as an executive secretary, a director of Christian education, and a director of world mission support. They have offices in the city, staffed with secretaries, and may issue a news letter monthly to keep the fellowship informed on current happenings. Some of the smaller associations, on the other hand, have very little organization and program, and their annual meetings are poorly attended. It is a matter of frequent discussion among Baptists whether efforts should be made toward the revitalization of associations, or toward abolishing them as outmoded by state conventions.

2. *State Conventions*

As a single association covers a limited extent of territory, it has been thought wise to have a more general organization, extending over and embracing the fields of all the associations in the state. This is called a Baptist state convention.

The convention is a missionary organization, interested in assisting and extending evangelical religion within the bounds of the state, in connection with the associations and churches. It works by helping the weaker churches and by supporting missionaries in neighborhoods of special need. State conventions also provide statewide leadership in Christian education and camping, evangelism, missionary promotion, care of the elderly, ministerial education, urban and rural church strategy, and many other fields. The executive secretary may serve as a "pastor to pastors," counseling and guiding them as they may require. He may also be of special help to pastorless churches

in providing them with names and supplementary
information concerning potential pastors and supply
preachers. In addition to the strictly spiritual culture
of their fields, state conventions assist and encourage
various educational institutions, especially denominational academies and schools for higher learning.

The meetings are held annually for two or three
days—one day being usually given to a state pastors'
conference. Reports are made by the associations,
addresses by missionaries and others, plans projected
for enlarged endeavors—special time and attention
being given to Christian education, evangelism, and
other special fields. The meetings alternate among
different sections of the state, and are held chiefly
in the larger communities, where facilities are adequate for the many who attend.

3. *National and Regional Groups*

The fellowship of Baptists on a national level is
far from unified, for there are many conventions of
varying natures transcending state lines. Four of
them—the American Baptist Churches, U.S.A., Southern Baptist Convention, National Baptist Convention of
America, and National Baptist Convention of the
U.S.A., Inc.,—include the vast majority of Baptists, with
memberships totaling almost twenty millions. Others
include groups who for one reason or another (often the
reason has been theological differences) have separated
themselves from the larger bodies; also groups which
have come from different national heritages (such as
German or Swedish) and have never united with the
others.

Listed below is a summary of all national Baptist groups claiming memberships of 50,000 or more, as reported in the 1964 edition of the *Yearbook of American Churches*:

American Baptist Association (1905), Texarkana, Ark.-Tex., a group of independent missionary Baptist churches, mainly in the south. Membership 653,000.

American Baptist Churches, U.S.A. (1907), Valley Forge, Pa., formerly the Northern Baptist Convention, with churches mainly in the northeastern, north central, and western states. Membership 1,544,505.

Baptist General Conference (1879), Chicago, Ill., formerly the Swedish Baptist General Conference. Membership 78,209.

Conservative Baptist Association of America (1947), Chicago and Wheaton, Ill., with churches mainly in northern and western states. Membership 300,000.

General Association of Regular Baptists (1932), Chicago, Ill., a fellowship of churches which withdrew from the Northern (American) Baptist Convention. Membership 148,416.

General Baptists (1907), an Arminian group of Baptists first organized by John Smyth and Thomas Helwys in England. Transplanted to the colonies in 1714, it died out along the seaboard but was revived in the midwest in 1823 by Rev. Benoni Stinson. Membership 60,423.

National Association of Free Will Baptists (1727), Nashville, Tenn. An Arminian Baptist group found in 34 states. Membership 193,664.

National Baptist Convention of America (1880), composed largely of Negro members. Membership 2,668,799.

National Baptist Convention of the U.S.A., Inc., the older and parent convention of Negro Baptists. Membership 5,000,000.[1]

National Baptist Evangelical Life and Soul Saving Assembly of the U.S.A. (1921), organized by A. A. Banks as a charitable, educational, and evangelical organization. Membership 57,674.

National Primitive Baptist Convention of the U.S.A. (1907), Huntsville, Ala., with churches located mainly in the southern states. Membership 85,983.

North American Baptist Association (1950), with churches mainly in the south and west. Membership 330,265.

North American Baptist General Conference, Forest Park, Ill., with churches of German background, throughout North America. Membership 52,073.

Primitive Baptists. A large group, mainly in the south, opposed to all centralization and to modern missionary societies. Membership 72,000.

Southern Baptist Convention (1845), Nashville, Tenn., at one time strictly a southern group but now spreading through the north. Membership 10,191,303.

United Baptists (1801), located in Kentucky and nearby states. Membership 63,641.

[1] In 1961, a group of churches from fourteen states withdrew from the National Baptist Convention of the U.S.A., Inc., to form the Progressive Baptist Convention of America.

The United Free Will Baptist Church (1870), Kinston, N. C., with churches located mainly in the Southeast. Membership 100,000.

The functions of these national conventions vary quite widely. The larger ones, as a rule, provide a means of conducting home and foreign mission work and a way of publishing curriculum materials for Christian education, and many of the smaller ones do the same. Other functions may include Christian social concern, evangelism, urban and rural church work, ministry to service men, Christian education program planning, ministerial pension fund, cooperation with schools, colleges, and campus Christian work, and many other services to the local church.

4. *Baptists of the World*

Although the overwhelming majority of Baptists are to be found in the United States, they may be found on all the continents in the world, and estimates as to their number usually come to about twenty-four millions. Not all the world's Baptists feel closely enough akin to one another to maintain fellowship, but the vast majority participate in the Baptist World Alliance, a rather loosely federated body established in 1905 which holds a world congress every five years (and a world youth congress during the intervening period) except when prevented from doing so by international tensions. The Baptist World Alliance also maintains a headquarters in Washington, D. C., through which various actions to strengthen the world fellowship of Baptists are taken from time to time.

5. Other Relationships

Some Baptist churches choose to maintain an inter-denominational fellowship through the large ecumenical bodies known as the National Council of the Churches of Christ in the U.S.A., the World Council of Churches, and the state and local councils which are related to these larger bodies. Others prefer a more restricted fellowship such as the National Association of Evangelicals, the American Council of Christian Churches, and the International Council of Christian Churches. Some will not associate as churches in any way with any non-Baptist churches, but do not object to their pastors' participation in interdenominational ministerial fellowships or other activities which do not involve the church as a whole. Still others object to any interdenominational fellowship at all. All in all, it must be said that Baptists have no single, clear voice in this matter, and that each church acts according to its own best understanding of the will of Christ.

CHAPTER VIII

CHURCH DISCIPLINE[1]

THE CHURCH is the school of Christ. As such, it should be controlled with wise and kindly discipline. The church is also a family; let there be law and order in the household, tempered with tenderness and discretion, otherwise the family fails of its mission, and becomes a reproach rather than a blessing to society. The church is the organic representative of the kingdom of Christ; unless law prevails in the kingdom and order is maintained, how shall the King be honored, the kingdom be advanced, or the world be blessed by its coming and triumph? It is therefore of the utmost importance that a correct scriptural discipline be strictly maintained within the churches.

[1] Disciplinary action on the part of churches is much less common than when Dr. Hiscox wrote his original chapter on the subject. Christian people today are less willing to sit in judgment than their forefathers. Nevertheless, at least on rare occasions, discipline may be necessary and desired. The present volume therefore contains in abridged form the principles and procedures which Dr. Hiscox recommended.

A. THREE LAWS OF CHRIST'S HOUSE

There are three laws of Christ's house, royal decrees, given by him who is "head over all things to the church," which stand invested with all the sanctions of divine authority:

First, for every disciple, the law of love. "A new commandment I give unto you, that ye love one another; as I have loved you, that ye also love one another" (John 13:34). This, if strictly obeyed, would prevent all cause of grief and offense, either personally to brethren or publicly to the church. It would prevent cold indifference to each other's welfare, unfounded suspicions, causeless accusations, jealousies, animosities, bitterness, hatred, and strife, and would cause each to love the other.

Second, for the offender, the law of confession. "If thou bring thy gift to the altar, and there rememberest that thy brother hath aught against thee, leave there thy gift before the altar, and go thy way; first be reconciled to thy brother, and then come and offer thy gift" (Matt. 5:23, 24). This law makes it obligatory on everyone who supposes that a brother has anything against him, to go to such a one without delay and secure, if possible, a reconciliation, whether there is in his opinion just cause or not for that brother to be offended.

Third, for the offended, the law of forgiveness. "If thy brother trespass against thee, rebuke him; and if he repent, forgive him. And if he trespass against thee seven times in a day, and seven times in a day turn again to thee, saying, I repent, thou shalt forgive him" (Luke 17:3, 4). This law requires a perpetual personal forgiveness of injuries, at least if those injuries are repented of and confessed. It does not require that one who has transgressed repeatedly should be held in the same esteem as before, for that might be impossible. In another form, the substance of this law was affirmed by Jesus, when, in answer to Peter's question as to how often one should forgive a brother, he replied, "I say not unto thee, Until seven times: but, Until seventy times seven" (Matt. 18:22). That is, constantly.

B. THE SCOPE OF DISCIPLINE

The object and purpose of discipline is to prevent, restrain, or remove the evil that may exist, to encourage and protect the right, and cherish the good, "for the edifying of the body of Christ," that it may be "perfect in love," and without reproach. That church is always held in higher esteem by its own members, and more respected and honored by the world, where a high standard of Christian morals is maintained, and a jealous watch-care is exercised over the faith and conduct of its members.

Discipline has a positive and definite purpose: to heal the offense if possible; or, failing this, to remove the offender. If the erring one can be induced to mend his ways, the desired result has been attained; that is, in all ordinary cases. Some exceptions may be hereafter mentioned. "If he repent, forgive him" (Luke 17:3).

Churches have a right and duty to exercise a watchful supervision over their members, to reprove them when erring, and to withdraw fellowship from them when incorrigible. This principle was recognized by Christ and his Apostles, and was exercised by the first churches. "Now we command you, brethren, in the name of our Lord Jesus Christ, that ye withdraw yourselves from every brother that walketh disorderly, and not after the tradition which he received of us" (2 Thess. 3:6). "A man that is an heretic after the first and second admonition, reject" (Titus 3:10).

The justification and effectiveness of discipline depend on the spirit in which it is exercised. It must not be exercised in a spirit of arrogance, nor of dictation, nor of assumed superiority, much less of vindictiveness, but of fraternal solicitude, of gentleness and love. Paul's injunction to the Galatians was, "Brethren, if a man be overtaken in a fault, ye which are spiritual restore such an one in the spirit of meekness; considering thyself lest thou also be tempted" (Gal. 6:1). These words should be written by the Spirit of God on every Christian heart. The work of restoration is to be done, in a spirit of meekness, with a sense of one's own liability to err.

The exercise of discipline is limited by the laws of Christ, kindly and generously interpreted, and by such matters of covenant agreement as were understood by each member on entering the church. On the other hand, matters which are purely personal to the individual, not violations of any law of the New Testament; not transgressions of Christian morals nor of covenant obligations, are not subject to discipline. Personal rights are to be held sacred, and no unauthorized yoke placed upon the necks of the disciples; no yoke but Christ's. "Now I praise you, brethren, that ye remember me in all things, and keep the ordinances, as I delivered them to you" (1 Cor. 11:2).

C. Dealing with Offenses

Offenses are usually considered as of two kinds, private and public (or personal and general):

1. Private Offenses

A private offense has reference to the personal relations of individual members, such as an injury done —or claimed to have been done—by one member to another, intentionally or unintentionally. It is personal, and rests between those two members alone. The course of treatment in all cases of private offenses is the one prescribed by our Savior in Matthew 18:15-17, consisting of three steps:

First step: "If thy brother shall trespass against thee, go and tell him his fault between thee and him alone; if he shall hear thee, thou hast gained thy brother." The one who considers himself injured must go to the offender, tell him his cause of grief, and between themselves alone adjust the matter, if possible, and settle the difficulty. It is the injured or offended one who goes to the offender, and not the reverse. The interview should be between themselves alone. No other persons should be present, either to help or to hinder, or to spread abroad the knowledge of the trouble. And the object must be to "gain his brother," not to humiliate, accuse, or condemn.

Second step: "But if he will not hear thee, then take with thee one or two more, that in the mouth of two or three witnesses every word may be established." If the previous step fails, the offended one must seek another interview with the offender, accompanied by one or two other members of the church, hoping to succeed where he himself alone had failed. He is not to abandon the effort with the failure of the first step, nor throw the responsibility of further effort on the offender. The object of taking the "one or two more" is chiefly that the church, should the matter come before them, may have witnesses, and not depend on the complainant, whose testimony very likely would be contradicted by the defendant. They could witness to the temper and spirit of the two, and to the facts, so far as ascertained. Moreover, they could act as mediators between the parties, and possibly aid in a friendly adjustment of the trouble without an appeal to the church.

Third step: "And if he shall neglect to hear them, tell it unto the church." Should the second attempt also be unsuccessful, the offended one must tell the whole matter to the church, which is to make the final decision after a full and fair hearing of the whole case. There is no higher tribunal, and no further appeal. The object all the way through is to "gain a brother." If, however, he will not show a brother's spirit, and will not act a brother's part, he is to be removed from the fellowship of the brotherhood.

2. *Public Offenses*

A public offense is one claimed to be a breach of Christian morals, or a violation of covenant faith or duty. It is not an offensive act committed against an individual, of which that individual might complain. It is an injury to the cause of piety, a scandal to the Christian name and profession. For instance, if it be credibly reported that a member is addicted to intemperance or profanity or dishonesty, or if he has departed from the faith or violated the order of the church in some grave matter, these are considered general, or public offenses, since in no sense are they personal or private in their commission or bearing.

In the treatment of public offenses, various cases have some peculiar features, and require peculiar treatments. The treatment of the case will therefore vary somewhat with the circumstances. Those who have the direction of them must be familiar with the general principles which apply:

1. The first member who has knowledge of the offense should, as in private cases, seek the offender, and, if possible, remove the difficulty. True, he is under no special obligation to do this simply because he chanced to be the first to learn the fact, but such would be a work of faith and a labor of love. Such personal efforts are often the most effectual. Should there be many individual efforts by many members at the same time, aiming at the same end, they would be so much the more effectual.

2. But if no one can or will pursue this course, or if it should prove unsuccessful, then the one who has

knowledge should consult the pastor and deacons, and leave it to their judgment as to what further course should be taken. All such cases should be kept out of church meetings and managed privately, so long as there seems hope of an effectual settlement by that means.

3. The pastor and deacons, having formal knowledge of the matter, would, perhaps, as the most kindly fraternal "first step" in their movement, visit him, hear his explanation and excuse, and ascertain his intentions. They should act in the name of the church and with its authority; but they should go in the spirit of meekness and love, with the desire uppermost to win a brother.

4. If the matter is not cleared up by this visit, the case should ultimately come before the church, where the offender shall know the charges, hear the witnesses, and be allowed to answer for himself. The church then renders its decision by vote.

5. If he will not appear before the church, by that refusal he defies its authority, and the body is free to act according to its best knowledge and judgment. If he be so situated that he cannot appear before them, they must depend on the report of a committee, and act according to their best judgment.

6. If, at any stage of the proceedings, the accused brother disproves the charges, or if he admits them, confesses the wrong, makes suitable acknowledgment and reparation, and promises to do better, this should be deemed sufficient, and the case be dismissed.

7. But if, after patient, deliberate, and prayerful labor, all efforts fail to reclaim the offender, then,

however painful the necessity, they must withdraw from him their fellowship.

Note 1.—Any one tried by a church should be allowed every opportunity, both as to time, place, and circumstance, to vindicate himself. The very justice of Christ's house should incline to mercy. It should be made manifest that the object is not to punish, but to reclaim.

Note 2.—The church should not commence disciplinary proceedings, nor even entertain a charge against a member, unless the evidence be such as to make the truth of the charge highly probable, if not absolutely certain.

Note 3.—The church should restore to its fellowship, at his request, any excluded member whenever it is satisfied with his present way of life and his confession and reparation for the past.

Note 4.—In all things not contrary to his conscience, the member should submit to the church, but in all questions of faith and conscience he should do what he honestly believes to be right, whether the church, in the exercise of administrative function, should commend or condemn him.

Note 5.—The relation of the pastor, to persons accused and to processes of trial before the body, is delicate and important. He is not to act the partisan for or against the accused, much less is to be the prosecutor of his erring brethren. Whatever may be his private opinion, he is to maintain fairness and equity on all sides and to all parties.

Note 6.—The moderator is to keep all parties in good order, and with just measures. It is important that he be familiar with parliamentary rules, and with the principles of scriptural discipline, so that the results reached shall commend themselves to the reasonable approval of all. In cases where he may himself be personally involved in the difficulty, he should not preside.

Note 7.—Certain special considerations are suggested for the discipline of pastors. See pages 65-69.

APPENDIX

THE NEW HAMPSHIRE
CONFESSION OF FAITH

I. THE SCRIPTURES

We believe that the Holy Bible was written by men divinely inspired, and is a perfect treasure of heavenly instruction; that it has God for its author, salvation for its end, and truth without any mixture of error for its matter; that it reveals the principles by which God will judge us; and therefore is, and shall remain to the end of the world, the true center of Christian union, and the supreme standard by which all human conduct, creeds, and opinions should be tried.

II. THE TRUE GOD

We believe the Scriptures teach that there is one, and only one, living and true God, an infinite, intelligent Spirit, whose name is Jehovah, the Maker and Supreme Ruler of heaven and earth; inexpressibly glorious in holiness, and worthy of all possible honor, confidence and love; that in the unity of the Godhead there are three persons, the Father, the Son, and the Holy Ghost; equal in every divine perfection, and executing distinct but harmonious offices in the great work of redemption.

III. THE FALL OF MAN

We believe the Scriptures teach that man was created in

137

holiness, under the law of his Maker; but by voluntary transgression fell from that holy and happy state; in consequence of which all mankind are now sinners, not by constraint but choice; being by nature utterly void of that holiness required by the law of God, positively inclined to evil; and therefore under just condemnation to eternal ruin, without defense or excuse.

IV. GOD'S PURPOSE OF GRACE

We believe the Scriptures teach that *election* is the eternal purpose of God, according to which he graciously regenerates, sanctifies and saves sinners; that being perfectly consistent with the free agency of man, it comprehends all the means in connection with the end; that it is a most glorious display of God's sovereign goodness, being infinitely free, wise, holy, and unchangeable; that it utterly excludes boasting, and promotes humility, love, prayer, praise, trust in God, and active imitation of his free mercy; that it encourages the use of means in the highest degree; that it may be ascertained by its effects in all who truly believe the Gospel; that it is the foundation of Christian assurance; and that to ascertain it with regard to ourselves demands and deserves the utmost diligence.

V. THE WAY OF SALVATION

We believe the Scriptures teach that the salvation of sinners is wholly of grace; through the mediatorial offices of the Son of God; who according to the will of the Father, assumed our nature, yet without sin; honored the divine law by his personal obedience, and by his death made a full atonement for our sins; that having risen from the dead, he is now enthroned in heaven; and uniting in his wonderful person the tenderest sympathies with divine perfections, he is every way qualified to be a suitable, a compassionate and an all-sufficient Savior.

VI. OF REGENERATION

We believe the Scriptures teach that *regeneration,* or the

new birth, is that change wrought in the soul by the Holy Spirit, by which a new nature and a spiritual life, not before possessed, are imparted, and the person becomes a new creation in Christ Jesus; a holy disposition is given to the mind, the will subdued, the dominion of sin broken, and the affections changed from a love of sin and self, to a love of holiness and God; the change is instantaneous, effected solely by the power of God, in a manner incomprehensible to reason; the evidence of it is found in a changed disposition of mind, the fruits of righteousness, and a newness of life. And without it salvation is impossible.

VII. OF REPENTANCE

We believe the Scriptures teach that *repentance* is a personal act, prompted by the Spirit; and consists in a godly sorrow for sin, as offensive to God and ruinous to the soul; that it is accompanied with great humiliation in view of one's sin and guilt, together with prayer for pardon; also by sincere hatred of sin, and persistent turning away from, and abandonment of, all that is evil and unholy. Since none are sinless in this life, repentance needs to be often repeated.

VIII. OF FAITH

We believe the Scriptures teach that *faith*, as an evangelical grace wrought by the Spirit, is the medium through which Christ is received by the soul as its sacrifice and Savior. It is an assent of the mind and a consent of the heart, consisting mainly of belief and trust; the testimony of God is implicitly accepted and believed as true, while Christ is unreservedly trusted for salvation; by it the believer is brought into vital relations with God, freely justified, and lives as seeing him who is invisible. Faith cannot save, but it reveals Christ to the soul as a willing and sufficient Savior, and commits the heart and life to him.

IX. OF JUSTIFICATION

We believe the Scriptures teach that the great gospel blessing which Christ secures to such as believe in Him is *justification*; that justification includes the pardon of sin, and the promise of eternal life on principles of righteousness; that it is bestowed, not in consideration of any works of righteousness which we have done, but solely through faith in the Redeemer's blood; by virtue of which faith his perfect righteousness is freely imputed to us of God; that it brings us into a state of most blessed peace and favor with God, and secures every other blessing needful for time and eternity.

X. OF ADOPTION

We believe the Scriptures teach that *adoption* is a gracious act, by which the Father, for the sake of Christ, accepts believers to the estate and condition of children, by a new and spiritual birth; sending the Spirit of adoption into their hearts, whereby they become members of the family of God, and entitled to all the rights, privileges, and promises of children; and if children, then heirs, heirs of God, and joint-heirs with Jesus Christ, to the heritage of the saints on earth, and an inheritance reserved in heaven for them.

XI. OF SANCTIFICATION

We believe the Scriptures teach that *sanctification* is the process by which, according to the will of God, we are made partakers of his holiness; that it is a progressive work; that it is begun in regeneration; that it is carried on in the hearts of believers by the presence and power of the Holy Spirit, the Sealer and Comforter, in the continual use of the appointed means—especially the Word of God, self-examination, self-denial, watchfulness, and prayer; and in the practice of all godly exercises and duties.

XII. THE PERSEVERANCE OF SAINTS

We believe the Scriptures teach that such as are truly regenerate, being born of the Spirit, will not utterly fall away and finally perish, but will endure unto the end; that their persevering attachment to Christ is the grand mark which distinguishes them from superficial professors; that a special Providence watches over their welfare; and they are kept by the power of God through faith unto salvation.

XIII. THE LAW AND THE GOSPEL

We believe the Scriptures teach that the Law of God is the eternal and unchangeable rule of his moral government; that it is holy, just, and good; and that the inability which the Scriptures ascribe to fallen men to fulfill its precepts arises entirely from their sinful nature; to deliver them from which, and to restore them through a Mediator to unfeigned obedience to the holy Law, is one great end of the Gospel, and of the means of grace connected with the establishment of the invisible Church.

XIV. A GOSPEL CHURCH

We believe the Scriptures teach that a visible Church of Christ is a congregation of baptized believers, associated by covenant in the faith and fellowship of the Gospel; observing the ordinances of Christ; governed by His laws; and exercising the gifts, rights, and privileges invested in them by his word; that its only scriptural officers are bishops or pastors and deacons, whose qualifications, claims, and duties are defined in the Epistles to Timothy and Titus.

XV. CHRISTIAN BAPTISM

We believe the Scriptures teach that Christian Baptism is the immersion in water of a believer in Christ, in the name of the Father, and Son, and Holy Ghost; to show forth, in a solemn and beautiful emblem, our faith in the crucified, buried, and risen Savior, with its effect, in our death to sin and resurrection to a new life; that it is prerequisite to the privileges of a church relation, and to the Lord's Supper.

XVI. THE LORD'S SUPPER

We believe the Scriptures teach that the Lord's Supper is

a provision of bread and wine, as symbols of Christ's body and blood, partaken of by the members of the church, in commemoration of the suffering and death of their Lord; showing their faith and participation in the merits of his sacrifice, and their hope of eternal life through his resurrection from the dead; its observance to be preceded by faithful self-examination.

XVII. THE CHRISTIAN SABBATH

We believe the Scriptures teach that the first day of the week is the Lord's Day; and is to be kept sacred to religious purposes, by abstaining from all secular labor, except works of mercy and necessity, by the devout observance of all the means of grace, both private and public; and by preparation for that rest that remaineth for the people of God.

XVIII. CIVIL GOVERNMENT

We believe the Scriptures teach that civil government is of divine appointment, for the interest and good order of human society; and that magistrates are to be prayed for, conscientiously honored and obeyed, except only in things opposed to the will of our Lord Jesus Christ, who is the only Lord of the conscience, and the Prince of the kings of the earth. But that civil rulers have no rights of control over, or of interference with, religious matters.

XIX. RIGHTEOUS AND WICKED

We believe the Scriptures teach that there is a radical and essential difference between the righteous and the wicked; that such only as through faith are justified in the name of the Lord Jesus, and sanctified by the Spirit of our God, are truly righteous in his esteem; while all such as continue in impenitence and unbelief are, in his sight, wicked and under the curse; and this distinction holds among men both in this life and after death.

XX. THE WORLD TO COME

We believe the Scriptures teach that the end of the world

is approaching; that at the last day, Christ will descend from heaven, and raise the dead from the grave for final retribution; that a solemn separation will then take place; that the wicked will be adjudged to endless sorrow, and the righteous to endless joy; and this judgment will fix forever the final state of men in heaven or hell, on principles of righteousness.

COVENANT

Having been, as we trust, brought by divine grace to embrace the Lord Jesus Christ, and to give ourselves wholly to him, we do now solemnly and joyfully covenant with each other, to walk together in him, with brotherly love, to his glory, as our common Lord. We do, therefore, in his strength, engage—

That we will exercise a Christian care and watchfulness over each other, and faithfully warn, exhort, and admonish each other as occasion may require:

That we will not forsake the assembling of ourselves together, but will uphold the public worship of God, and the ordinances of his house:

That we will not omit closet and family religion at home, nor neglect the great duty of religiously training our children, and those under our care, for the service of Christ, and the enjoyment of heaven:

That, as we are the light of the world, and salt of the earth, we will seek divine aid to enable us to deny ungodliness, and every worldly lust, and to walk circumspectly in the world, that we may win the souls of men:

That we will cheerfully contribute of our property, according as God has prospered us, for the maintenance of a faithful and evangelical ministry among us, for the support of the poor, and to spread the Gospel over the earth:

That we will in all conditions, even till death, strive to live to the glory of him who hath called us out of darkness into his marvelous light.

"And may the God of Peace, who brought again from the dead our Lord Jesus, that great shepherd of the sheep, through the blood of the everlasting covenant, make us perfect in every good work, to do his will, working in us that which is well pleasing in his sight through Jesus Christ; to whom be glory, forever and ever. Amen."

The New Hampshire Confession was prepared by a committee appointed by the New Hampshire Baptist Convention and was adopted by that body in 1833. At a later date Dr. J. Newton Brown added an article on repentance and faith and one on sanctification. Dr. Hiscox further revised the confession to its present form, including the article on adoption, which he wrote himself. The text as printed here is Dr. Hiscox's final version.